"Jennifer Kvamme answers stude[...] diffi[...] questions with
the deep compassion that comes [...] two decades of dedicated
next-generation ministry. She infuses every page with a personal
freshness that relates to the real-life struggles and highest joys of
a teenager's world. Guided by the whole story of God's word, this
book is a trustworthy map that leads students to discover joy and
freedom in God's wonderful design for human connection."

DR. KEN CASTOR, NEXT-GENERATION PASTOR AND AUTHOR

"This book manages to be wise, persuasive, warm, and sensitive
in answering the hardest questions, in a hopeful and helpful way.
A great resource for giving away, but also worth keeping in your
back pocket!"

LINDA ALLCOCK, AUTHOR, "HEAD, HEART, HANDS" BIBLE NOTES

"Our culture's story around gender, sex, and identity is told loudly
and often enough to be compelling to those hearing it. But, as
Jennifer Kvamme wisely and winsomely demonstrates, God has
another, better story for us. This is an easily accessible, up-to-
date, and compassionate take on our culture's false promises that
we can find true satisfaction in things that are good but which are
not ultimate. Written in an engaging and down-to-earth style, it's
perfectly pitched to answer the burning questions young people
are asking. That it does so with humility, grace, openness, and
a genuine sense of inquiry makes it a safe, sage book in these
bewildering times."

STEPHEN MCALPINE, AUTHOR, "BEING THE BAD GUYS: HOW
TO LIVE FOR JESUS IN A WORLD THAT SAYS YOU SHOULDN'T"

"These are the issues where our teenage children most need help.
That help has arrived! This book tells the better story about sex,
gender, and sexuality that our teenagers desperately need to hear.
Thank you, Jennifer!"

ED DREW, DIRECTOR, FAITH IN KIDS; AUTHOR, "RAISING CONFIDENT KIDS"

"Clear and gracious, this book shows how God's story of redemption and a committed relationship with Jesus are the foundation for making sense of some of the most important questions young people are facing today. An essential read for teens and young adults. Pastors, youth workers, parents, and grandparents will also benefit greatly from this well-written explanation of God's perspective on these significant issues."

KEVIN KOMPELIEN, PRESIDENT, EVANGELICAL FREE CHURCH OF AMERICA

"Full of compassion and grace, truth and love, Jennifer paints a better picture—a glorious picture—of God's good design. This book will be a catalyst for desires to become realigned with the heart of God."

KRISTEN HATTON, AUTHOR,
"FACE TIME: YOUR IDENTITY IN A SELFIE WORLD"

"Every pastor, every youth worker, every parent needs to read this powerful conversation tool as they wrestle honestly with reaching and discipling this generation. These are conversations that need to be had, and Jennifer approaches them with clear, compassionate biblical wisdom."

DOUG HOLLIDAY, PRESIDENT, SONLIFE MINISTRIES

"This book is an essential read for those who are feeling lost or uncertain about their true self, or for those seeking deeper understanding of their purpose according to God's plan."

RENNIE GARDA, CADRE DISCIPLEMAKING MISSIONARY

"For the person who desires more clarity about God's perspective, purpose, and plan, this book builds a foundation of how to think about God and self. I am thankful that there is more to the story that God invites us to embrace and live out. I highly recommend this book!"

GLENN OLSON, DIRECTOR OF STUDENT MINISTRIES,
NORTH CENTRAL DISTRICT EFCA

"*More to the Story* is such an important book. Jennifer talks about some of the most challenging topics of the day—body, gender, dating, abuse—in such a clear manner. There's so much that's helpful in this accessible resource. A vital book for parents and youth workers to put in the hands of their pre-teen, teen, or older."

JOHN PERRITT, DIRECTOR OF RESOURCES, REFORMED YOUTH MINISTRIES

"This is an important discussion for students right now (and adults too), and Jennifer is the right person to address it. Writing with years of experience as a youth worker and with commitment to the gospel, she addresses this topic through the lens of who God is and who we are in him. I recommend getting this book into the hands of any student in your life!"

LAURIE SEAY, EVENT DIRECTOR, EFCA

"I knew that the Bible's standpoint on sex and relationships was different from the world's, but this book really helped me understand why God views sex in the way he does, why it's so special, and why the world's view is so far out of line with God's design for humanity."

KATE, 18

"This book helped me see what kids at school might be thinking or feeling, and gave me language to show love to people walking a different road than me. And yet it stayed true to God's word."

RANI, 15

"The book makes you realise and appreciate why sexuality and everything that comes with it is so important to God. It puts our world's ideas into context by giving us a bigger, more godly picture. It's worth reading because you can reality-check your own thinking."

JACK, 17

"If we realise that our fascination with romance is actually a memory-trace of a deeper story—an echo of a greater tune, a signpost to the ultimate destination—then we will find the reality that can transcend even the most intimate of relationships we can experience."

— Sam Allberry [1]

MORE TO THE STORY

Jennifer M. Kvamme

thegoodbook
COMPANY

To Greg,
whose steadfast, selfless love
daily paints me a living picture of Jesus.

— J.M.K.

More to the Story
© Jennifer M. Kvamme, 2024

Published by:
The Good Book Company

thegoodbook.com | thegoodbook.co.uk
thegoodbook.com.au | thegoodbook.co.nz | thegoodbook.co.in

ISBN: 9781784989514 | JOB-007405 | Printed in Turkey

Design by Drew McCall

Contents

Start Here

I WONDER WHAT BROUGHT YOU to this book.

Maybe you love following Jesus and you want to know what he really says about sexuality—or how to explain his teachings to your friends. Maybe you find the Bible's teachings on sex offensive, and you come to this book skeptical. Or maybe you bring some deep pain. Maybe just having a female or male body is a constant source of discomfort, or you wonder if God hates you because you're gay. Maybe you feel shame around your sexuality, and you want to know if there's hope. Or maybe you just want to know why sex is such a big deal to Christians!

The Bible has gotten a bad rap lately when it comes to its teachings on sexuality. I mean, if you asked the average teen in your school what the Bible had to say about sex, what do you think they'd say? When I've asked students, the most common response I get is "Don't do it." Not exactly captivating.

Meanwhile, our culture is telling a story more like this: "You can be whoever you want to be, love whoever you want to love, and use your body however you want. Sex is fun, and it's no big deal. No one else can tell you who you are or who to love. Just respect everyone."

It's pretty clear which message sounds more like good news.

Here's the deal, though: I absolutely believe that the Bible's message about sex, attraction, identity, and relationships is *by far* the better news. And it saddens me that too often it hasn't been communicated like that. When people hear condemnation, or a weighty list of "don't"s, and leave burdened (or proud), they're missing the heart of God. And if this has been your experience, I'm so sorry.

You see, it really isn't just "Don't do it." When the Bible talks about sex and related topics, it's not primarily through a list of rules and warnings. It's through a story. That story doesn't shy away from the darkness and brokenness of life, but it's ultimately full of good news for the longings of our hearts and bodies.

HOW TO READ THIS BOOK

You've probably looked at the contents page already. You know which questions you want answers to, and you're likely tempted to skip ahead to particular chapters and find out what the Bible has to say about dating, or porn, or gay and trans issues. I get that—but let me ask you to resist that urge for now. The chapters build on each other, and in particular I really, *really* don't want you to miss the first three chapters. Because I don't just want to give you rules to follow. I want to introduce you to a story—and a person—that has transformed me and many, many others. And I believe that if you can pause long enough to listen to the story God is telling, you'll hear of something much bigger and more beautiful than you dreamed.

So, here's the important thing: read the first three chapters first.

One more note: at the end of every chapter you'll find a couple of reflection questions. Those are intended to help you think through what you've read for yourself. You might also want to use them to help you chat about your thoughts with a friend or a trusted adult, or to journal about them. Then, at the end of the book, there's a discussion guide—this is a bit more in-depth and designed to work best in groups. You'll also find a list of recommended resources if you want to delve further into one of the topics raised in the book.

> **"I WANT TO INTRODUCE YOU TO A STORY THAT HAS TRANSFORMED ME AND MANY OTHERS."**

It's possible this book won't answer all your questions. I couldn't cover everything! Or maybe you're not convinced by what I'm telling you. That's actually ok with me. My hope is that it will lead you to dig into the Bible for yourself to see if what I'm telling you is true or to find answers to other questions. Ultimately, I pray it will show you that Jesus is good, that he can be trusted, and that following him is worth whatever he asks of us.

THERE'S MORE TO THE STORY

I've been working with teens at my church for 20 years, and I've been privileged to be a part of many of their stories. I've watched middle schoolers grow into adults, listened as they shared their deepest struggles and highest joys, and seen Jesus heal pain and transform lives. I've heard their questions about God, life, and yes, sex. And I've grieved as I watched students walk away from the church because they sensed judgment and exclusion and didn't see how Jesus could be good news for them. That's what led me to write this book.

Here's what I've seen: everyone craves acceptance, connection, and love. We want people to see us, to know us deeply, and to love us fully. That's hardwired into us as humans, even though that kind of love can feel elusive.

But here's what not everyone realizes: this longing for love and connection is by design. It's part of what it means to be human! And as with anything, understanding the meaning and purpose of its design tells us how to make the best use of our sexuality.

The truth is that there is more going on in our gender than biology, and more to sex than pleasure and connection. We're all looking for a relationship that will satisfy, but the Bible tells us that only God satisfies—and all our longings and desires are supposed to lead us to him.

That might sound pretty weird at this point. I get that. But in order to uncover the better news about sexuality that the Bible has to offer, we need to start with the story of God.

An Eternal Echo

SEXUALITY AS A GLIMPSE OF SOMETHING DEEPER

IMAGINE YOU MEET SOMEONE NEW at school this year—the most attractive person you've ever known. He or she seems to be attracted to you, too, and before long, romance has blossomed. This person loves listening to you and getting to know your heart; they make you laugh and make your heart thrill, and before long you share all your deepest secrets... and they love you even more for it. They constantly plan romantic surprises, speak well of you in front of your friends, buy you the most meaningful gifts, and promise they're going to be there for you forever.

It's the stuff of fairy tales, the happy-ever-after ending. Deep down you probably know this kind of perfection isn't real. But isn't there still a part of you that wants it to be true?

We long to be known. We want to be seen for who we really are and loved without condition. We want someone else to know deeply, to share life with, to adventure with, to talk with about anything—someone who is just *there*. Our hearts have an insatiable craving for intimacy.

And, actually, so do our bodies. We've all experienced the sight—or touch—of someone who made our heart beat a little faster. Maybe you've felt the full-on physical pull of your body to be connected to someone else. There's little doubt, even from a purely scientific look at our physical design, that our bodies were made for intimacy with another... even if the details of *who* and *when* and *how* have less agreement.

What we're about to see is that all of this is *good*. It's by design. God made our bodies and our hearts to crave intimacy and togetherness. God was the one who thought up sex and romance.

But what we're also going to see is *why* God designed us that way. Spoiler alert: your sexuality was intended to show you how intensely he loves you.

A PERFECT DESIGN

In the first chapter of the Bible, God begins with nothing and creates everything. And he does so with amazing intentionality, creativity, and order. Day one, he says, "Let there be light," and there is light. He calls it good and separates the light from darkness, and there's evening and morning—the first day.

So begins a pattern for all of creation. God makes something new—something from his own imagination and design, without consulting anyone or using any materials—and then creates a boundary for it. He makes sky and separates it from the waters below. He makes dry ground, separates it from the seas, and fills it with plants. He makes lights in the sky to separate day from night and mark seasons and years. He creates sea creatures for the water and birds for the skies and animals for the land, and all of it is good.

But it was all setting things up for the climax of his work: people. "So God created man in his own image, in the image of God he created him" (Genesis 1:27). Humans were an intentional, culminating masterpiece of God's creation. We were his idea. From the mind-blowing detail of how our eyes and brains work to the practicality of fingernails and opposing thumbs—and yes, the design of our gender and sexuality—all of it was God's ingenuity. And he delighted in it. He called the creation of humanity *very* good.

But then came the first time God said something was *not* good. Initially he created only one human, a man; and it was not good for the man to be alone (2:18).

This wasn't an oversight in God's perfect design. He didn't create Adam, watch him for a while, and then realize that Adam was lonely. Adam's need for another person was no surprise to God. It was all part of his plan.

And so he put Adam to sleep, took a rib from his side, and built a woman. Eve was "fit for" him (v 18). She was a custom-made match, just perfect, just what he'd been missing and didn't know he needed.

Here's where sexuality comes into the design. God gave the first man life, created the first woman custom-fitted for him, and then gave them both the gift of marriage. And within this gift of marriage (drumroll, please...) we find sex introduced. God talks about the man and the woman becoming "one flesh" (v 24). In other words, the "fit" between Adam and Eve was not just relational and spiritual—it was also physical. The bodies of a man and a woman are designed to fit together in sex. And this act is meant to draw two people into a union that is the closest of human relationships. In sex you become one flesh, and that relationship is intended to be lifelong. (This, by the way, is why Christians say sex should be kept for marriage.)

Do you know what God's first command to his newly created people was? "Be fruitful and multiply" (1:28). He was talking about sex. His very first command wasn't *Don't do it* but *Do it—a lot!* God wanted his people to enjoy the good gift he'd given them and, in turn, to be creators with him of more humans.

Adam immediately recognized this as something to be celebrated, something wonderfully good. When he first saw Eve, he joyously responded with a poem, or a love song:

> *"This at last is bone of my bones*
> *and flesh of my flesh;*
> *she shall be called Woman,*
> *because she was taken out of Man." (2:23)*

So here we have Adam and Eve, together, naked, and without shame (v 25). Their bodies are designed to be a reason for celebration, a gift to one another. Sex, as God created it, is meant to be full of joy and free from shame. There is perfect intimacy, closeness, nakedness, without fear or guilt or manipulation. There's no embarrassment, selfishness, or flaunting. Adam and Eve are together, nothing between them, nothing to hide, full of delight.

Of course, this is not the reality you and I are familiar with today. Adam and Eve's relationship is the ideal marriage, but this perfect, shame-free fitting together of a man and a woman is not how most human relationships turn out—even the good ones. We'll get to why in the next chapter, but for now let me say that just because we sometimes find our experiences of sexuality much more complex and difficult than Adam and Eve did, it doesn't mean we should dismiss God's good design. This is super important—because God's plan for sexuality isn't just about sexuality. The perfect human marriage was good, but it was not God's endgame.

HINTS OF MORE

Sometimes we need something we can see and touch to help us understand an idea. The diagrams in science books are important, aren't they? My husband is an engineer for a nuclear power plant, and there are definitely times he has to stop his explanation and sketch me a picture so I can track with the conversation.

God loves sketching his people pictures, too! And sexuality and marriage are among the most powerful pictures we have. They're God's way of helping us understand the intimacy we can have with him.

> "THE PERFECT HUMAN MARRIAGE WAS GOOD, BUT IT WAS NOT GOD'S ENDGAME."

To see why, let's go back to Genesis. The first time the Bible tells us people had sex, it says, "Now Adam knew Eve his wife, and she conceived and bore Cain" (4:1). You could say "knew" is a polite way to say "had sex with" because God was trying to keep things PG. But if you read the rest of the Bible, it's pretty clear that keeping things PG isn't what God is after. The word "knew" is significant. Sex brings a deep, intimate kind of knowledge of each other's bodies—and, in the context of a marriage between two people over the long haul, an intimate knowing of their whole persons.

But it's more significant even than that. The same Hebrew word, *yada*, is used in Psalm 139:1 when King

David says, "O LORD, you have searched me and known me!" God knows us perfectly, and he desires for us to know him intimately. The deep "knowing" found in sex is a picture of our relationship with him.

Let me be really clear: I'm not saying our relationship with God is in any way sexual! That would be unbiblical, not to mention creepy. But our sexuality is one way God helps us understand just how fully he knows us, how deeply he cherishes us, and how passionately he desires for us to return his love. This means that the most important thing to understand about sex and marriage isn't actually the one-flesh lifelong commitment we've seen already—important though that is. It's that sex—and marriage—are not ultimate. *Marriage is not the deepest possible intimacy nor sex the most intense possible pleasure.* (Yes, go ahead and read that sentence again. It's true!) Marriage and sex—even at their best—are faint shadows of something infinitely greater: the relationship with God for which we were ultimately designed.

I know, I know. You're a little skeptical on that. But hang with me and let's see how the Bible has been showing us this from beginning to end.

GOD'S UNFAITHFUL WIFE

The themes of intimacy, faithfulness, and love aren't just abstract concepts in the Bible; they repeatedly play out in the storyline of God and his people. God frequently describes his chosen people, Israel, as his "wife." Nowhere is this metaphor more clear than in the story of Hosea.

Hosea was a man in Old Testament times who got a big (and really personal) glimpse of God's metaphor of marriage. God gave him a surprising command: *Go, marry someone who's promiscuous and sure to be unfaithful to you. I've got something to teach my people* (Hosea 1:2). Hosea did exactly that. He picked a woman named Gomer. And guess what? After they had had a couple kids together, she left him and started sleeping around with other men. *Umm... what are you up to, God?* Think of the heartache for Hosea and these kids! Why would God command such a thing?

(Side note: Hosea was given a unique task by God. Don't take it as general marriage advice!)

Well, God told him why: "For like an adulterous wife this land is guilty of unfaithfulness to the LORD" (v 2, NIV). In other words, Hosea's wife was just like the people of God: unfaithful to the one they had pledged to love forever, the one who had always been faithful to them. Hosea, through his heartbreaking marriage, was showing the people something about themselves.

And, as it turns out, something about God. Because here's what we see in Hosea 3:1:

> *"Go again, love a woman who is loved by another man and is an adulteress, even as the Lord loves the children of Israel, though they turn to other gods."*

Just as before, Hosea obeyed. He had to buy back his own wife out of prostitution, but she returned to live with him. In doing this, Hosea displayed to the whole nation of Israel something about the character of God.

God loves his people (which meant Israel then, and means Christians now) like a husband loves his bride. And he is faithful, even if we are not. Even when we rely on ourselves and ignore God. Or we flat-out disobey his commands and disbelieve his word. Like a wounded husband who just keeps wooing his bride, God doesn't give up on us but actively seeks us out. No matter the cost.

That's beautiful... and a little crazy. I mean, would we counsel someone whose wife became a prostitute to go pay the fee and bring her back? Maybe cut your losses and move on, right? But not God.

Do you see the point? The deep feelings and intense experiences that go with human sexuality are supposed to tell us about God's love for us. The pain we feel when someone is unfaithful is a tiny picture of the wrenching pain he feels when we turn away from him. The wonder we feel when a spouse loves us in our weaknesses and forgives us when we hurt them is a small glimpse of what it is like to experience God's unceasing tenderness. He designed our sexuality to show us how much he loves us.

THE ULTIMATE BRIDEGROOM

While there are moments like that, likening God to a husband, throughout the Old Testament, it's not until the New Testament that we learn that, all along, marriage has been doing something even more. It's been pointing to Jesus. In Ephesians 5, the apostle Paul is giving married couples instructions about how to treat one another—and in the middle, he quotes from the story of Adam and Eve in Genesis 2, reminding us that marriage is rooted in the creation story: "Therefore a man shall leave his father and mother and hold fast to his wife, and the two shall become one flesh." Next, he gives the meaning of that familiar story an astonishing twist by saying, "This mystery is profound, and I am saying that it refers to Christ and the church" (Ephesians 5:31-32).

Paul is claiming that, all along, Genesis 2's "one flesh" idea was really talking about Jesus and his followers. That somehow, the uniting that happens between a husband and a wife—and the deep intimacy and commitment they share—is in a profound way like the relationship Christians have with Jesus. He's the ultimate bridegroom.

This has big practical implications. Jesus sacrificed his life for his church, and marriages are meant to reflect the same kind of love. Our sexual relationships are supposed to be enduring, committed "one flesh" arrangements— each partner upholding and making sacrifices for the other. It's not just about what we can get but about what we can give. If you're wondering why Christians take marriage so seriously, this is why: it's supposed to show off something about Jesus' love for his followers, the most important love we've ever known.

We'll get more into the practicalities of this in future chapters, but for now what God wants us to see is that sexuality is more significant than you might have realized. Sex is a good gift. But it's not ultimate. It's meant to point us to and prepare us for an eternal marriage of Christ with his people. It's meant to show us, in a tangible way, the amazing faithful, sacrificial, passionate love of Jesus for his people—and to woo us back to him when we stray. This was God's grand vision when he designed our bodies back in Genesis 1.

But as we follow this story of God's relationship with his people, we're not quite ready to get to Jesus yet. There's something else we need to see first. The story starts with the joyful intimacy of Eden, which is meant to paint us a picture of God's love. It will end in eternity with the perfect marriage of Christ and his people. But in between, the storyline is about to take a sharp turn. If your experience of attraction, sexual identity, or physical intimacy doesn't match what's been described in this chapter—if you've experienced pain, confusion, or condemnation—the next act of the story will help you understand just what went wrong, and why there's still great hope.

FOR REFLECTION

WE READ THAT "YOUR SEXUALITY WAS INTENDED TO SHOW YOU HOW INTENSELY [GOD] LOVES YOU."

- DOES THIS DESCRIPTION OF THE DEEP LOVE OF CHRIST RING TRUE FOR YOU?

- IN WHAT WAYS HAVE YOU EXPERIENCED THAT LOVE?

- CONSIDER TURNING YOUR REACTION TO THIS SENTENCE INTO A PRAYER TO GOD, INVITING HIM TO SHOW YOU THE DEPTH OF HIS LOVE.

"GOD'S PLAN FOR SEXUALITY ISN'T JUST ABOUT SEXUALITY."

- WHAT IS IT ABOUT?

- DOES THIS MAKE YOU THINK ABOUT YOUR OWN SEXUALITY, RELATIONSHIPS, OR ATTRACTIONS IN A DIFFERENT WAY?

An Ancient Lie

THE ENEMY WHO WORKS TO SABOTAGE AND DESTROY WHAT'S GOOD

SEVERAL YEARS AGO I WAS in Galveston, Texas, shortly after Hurricane Ike ripped through the area. The damage left in its wake, even two months later, was a bit surreal. Homes built on stilts leaned dangerously to the side. Others had been torn apart, and wreckage was lying on the ground. Shops and restaurants were boarded up, leaving parts of town eerily vacant. Homeless people begged for help. The amount of devastation brought on by a single event was sobering.

But Hurricane Ike's destruction pales dramatically in comparison with that of another single event long before. According to the Bible, *all* of the devastation, brokenness, pain, and frustration in the world can be traced, in one way or another, back to a single moment. We call that event "the fall." It's the first time humans chose sin over God. And understanding just what went wrong that fateful day (and how it still affects us today) is essential if we want to make sense of life—and of all the questions and issues related to sex and sexuality.

After all, the picture we've painted so far of sex is really beautiful. But chances are, you've seen its ugly side. Maybe you've experienced the horror of being forced into a sexual experience you didn't want. Maybe you're plagued by guilt over choices you've made or images you've seen (or sent) on your phone. Maybe you are tired of battling the temptations in your mind. Maybe your own body or gender is a source of pain. To make sense of the brokenness that is so often a part of our experiences of sexuality, we have to understand the fall.

Remember, as a backdrop to the story, that God had just created Adam and Eve as the first humans and placed them in a garden that was quite literally paradise. They had an abundance of everything they'd ever need: a lovely home, plenty of food, peace and safety. They had a perfect marriage. They walked with God personally and heard his voice. What else could they possibly desire?

EVIL ENTERS THE SCENE

But a fourth character enters the story in Genesis 3:1. A crafty serpent approaches Eve and asks, "Did God actually say, 'You shall not eat of any tree in the garden'?"

The question is ridiculous in its error. God had abundantly provided for his children, giving them not just one kind of food but a garden full of fruit trees to delight their taste buds and fill their stomachs. But within that free choice was a warning that there was one tree to avoid:

> "You may surely eat of every tree of the garden, but of the tree of the knowledge of good and evil you

> shall not eat, for in the day that you eat of it you
> shall surely die." (2:16-17)

That seems like a pretty good reason to avoid it! I don't let my kids pick any mushrooms that grow in the woods, even though they might be healthy delicacies, because I know some mushrooms are deadly and I don't want to risk my kids' lives. If we were picking apples in an orchard and the farmers warned me that one particular tree was poisonous, we'd stay far away. In the same way, God warns his children that, among all the delicious and nutritious fruits in the garden, there's one lone tree they must avoid or else risk their lives. Simple enough, right?

But along comes this snake, this deceiver, with a question: "Did God actually say...?"

Eve, of course, knows what God actually said. Here's how she responds to the serpent:

> "We may eat of the fruit of the trees in the garden,
> but God said, 'You shall not eat of the fruit of the
> tree that is in the midst of the garden, neither
> shall you touch it, lest you die.'" (3:2-3)

Is that what God said? Sort of. She gets the first part right, about being free to eat from the trees in the garden (though she leaves out the word "all"). But when she recounts God's command about the tree, she neglects to call it by its name, and she oddly adds the part about not touching it, which God *hadn't* said. Perhaps it's a rule Adam and Eve had given themselves, to make certain they avoided that tree. I mean, if you don't touch it, you can't eat it, so they might have thought they were adding an additional layer of safety.

Unfortunately, it wasn't the kind of safety layer they needed.

The serpent responds with the first all-out lie in Scripture:

> *"You will not surely die. For God knows that when you eat of it your eyes will be opened, and you will be like God, knowing good and evil." (v 4)*

The thing is, Adam and Eve had already been made in God's image and pronounced "very good" by their Creator. They already were "like God" in the best possible way. They already had the full experience of *good* in this perfect garden. All that they lacked was a knowledge of evil—and we all know they were better off without that!

But the serpent's words were enough to cause the woman to take another look at this forbidden, deadly fruit. The seeds of doubt in God, in his words, and in his goodness were already in her heart. And when she looked at the fruit, it looked good.

So she ate.

Adam, apparently, had been with her all along (v 6), and he didn't speak up to protect her or remind her of God's goodness and his word. Instead, he ate it, too.

And their eyes were opened—but not in the way they'd hoped. They now had a knowledge of evil, from experience, and it immediately affected their sexuality. When they looked at their bodies, they saw nakedness, and they wanted to hide (v 7).

They had always been naked, and before, it had been a source of delight. (Remember Adam's joyful poetry upon first seeing Eve?) They had felt safe, comfortable in their own skin and with each other. They had never had any reason to be afraid or ashamed. But now, with this new knowledge of evil, they saw danger all around them, including in each other. They huddled in the garden, sewing leaves together to cover up their bodies—their bodies that had been made gloriously in the image of God.

RIPPLE EFFECTS

At that moment, it was like the foundation of the world began to crack, and soon small fissures spread in every direction. God told Adam and Eve that because of their sin, they could not stay in the garden. They would instead have to work the ground, which would now produce thorns and make their labor difficult. In the very next chapter of Genesis, their first son murders his brother out of jealousy. In the same chapter, we see the first instance of polygamy and a man bragging about killing someone who injured him. By chapter 6, "The Lord saw that the wickedness of man was great in the earth, and that every intention of the thoughts of his heart was only evil continually" (6:5). Soon there is abuse, slavery, gang rape, adultery, prostitution, murder, and war—and that's just the first book of the Bible. (I told you it wasn't PG!)

The fall began unraveling the good of God's created design. It affected humans' closest relationships (with God and each other), their bodies, their work, and their home. Pain, frustration, conflict, struggle, and death had now entered the world, and they would continue their destructive work throughout the millennia to come.

None of us have escaped unscathed from sin's destruction. Everything we touch is now damaged in some way. In fact, even if we look solely at the area of sexuality, we've all been affected. All of us experience some level of pain or difficulty in our sexuality because of the fall—including in ways that aren't our choice or our fault.

It looks different for each of us. Some of us have bodies that don't work the way they're intended to. Some of us have an overwhelming sense of distress and discomfort about our bodies because we feel like they've been made with the wrong gendered parts. Some of us find ourselves filled with desires we didn't ask for and don't want... or we *don't* experience sexual desires, and we wish we did. Some of us find ourselves the victims of others' cruel desires. Some of us, without any history of trauma, still feel shame and discomfort whenever our sexuality is mentioned. And some of us know that we've been the cause of pain. The choices we've made have hurt others, or we've done things against our own bodies that we regret. For all of us, the perfect intimacy God designed, free of fear or shame or awkwardness, has been shattered.

At some level, all of us are out of sync with God, creation, each other, and our own bodies. All of creation (including our very selves) has been subjected to futility, according to Romans 8:20. In other words, as long as we live in a fallen world, there will always be a yearning for something more, a frustration.

That's because hardwired into each of us at our creation is an innate sense that we were created for something different. "[God] has planted eternity in the human heart," wrote Solomon in Ecclesiastes 3:11 (NLT).

> "AT SOME LEVEL, ALL OF US ARE OUT OF SYNC WITH GOD, CREATION, EACH OTHER, AND OUR OWN BODIES."

Something deep inside us knows that this is not all as it ought to be. We were created to be in perfect relationship with God and with each other. Our sexuality was a gift meant to be life-giving, experienced in faithful and sacrificial love—and it was meant to point us to the depth and steadfastness of God's love for us. It was not meant for pain, shame, or anxiety.

THE NATURE OF SIN

Is it hard to believe that all of the destruction, pain, and violence we experience is a consequence of two people's choice to eat a certain fruit? I mean, if we were to list out all of the possible sins a person could commit and rank them from "completely awful" to "fairly insignificant," I'm going to guess that murder and abuse would be at the top and eating a fruit you were told not to eat would be near the bottom of the list. What was the big deal with this particular fruit?

Perhaps this reasoning reveals that we think about sin differently than God does—and we don't truly understand what it is. We tend to think of sin as doing something wrong, disobeying a commandment. That's partly true. But at a more significant level, sin is about worship. It's about what we most treasure and whom we most trust. What God is after is not simply that we follow his instruction but that we trust his heart.

The serpent's words created doubt in Eve's mind. She wondered if maybe God was holding out on her—maybe he didn't really have her best interests in mind. Perhaps the tree he had forbidden would give her power, and God was trying to keep it for himself. She wasn't sure anymore.

And instead of looking to God and asking herself whether he was trustworthy and good, she looked at the tree. She saw that the forbidden fruit was "good for food … a delight to the eyes, and … to be desired to make one wise" (Genesis 3:6). What's interesting is that God never said it wasn't. In fact, when he looked at everything he'd made, including that tree, he called it good. But Eve's estimation of what was ultimately good was at odds with God's instructions.

Jackie Hill Perry, in her book *Gay Girl, Good God*, writes, "The tree was indeed good for food and pleasant to the sight; God had made it that way ... The deception was in believing that the tree was more satisfying to the body and more pleasurable to the sight than God."[2] Eve's primary sin wasn't just disobedience but unbelief, which leads to a misplacement of our deepest love.

The original sin wasn't really about fruit. It was about obedience, but it was much more than that. It was about worship. It was about what Adam and Eve most valued. And it was about whom they trusted. When they looked at the juicy fruit hanging up on that tree, they were no longer satisfied with God and what he had given them. That fruit seemed, in that moment, more delightful than God. They had the choice to trust what God had told them or what their eyes saw, and they deemed their senses more reliable indicators of what was true and good than the words of God.

They failed to believe God's word, failed to trust his heart, failed to view him as their highest value, and in so doing, they worshiped created things rather than their Creator. They trusted themselves rather than their God.

Which is exactly the same sin we are tempted with every day.

It's probably not about fruit; we don't live in Eden. But we are regularly faced with a similar choice: will we trust God and love him supremely, or will we trust our own perception and choose our own way? God commands us to honor our parents, but their rules are so maddening! God wants our conversations to be full of grace, but it feels good to vent our frustrations. God instructs us not to lust, but the thrill of looking at porn draws us to pull out our phones at night. God calls us to reserve sex for marriage, but our bodies want it now. And so we, like Adam and Eve, frequently question, "Did God really say...?" Like them, we often choose to believe our hearts and our senses more than the word of God. In doing so, we declare who has our allegiance and our trust—and it's not our Creator. Even committed Christians are too often the unfaithful bride turning away from God to chase other loves.

To fight sin, we usually focus on behavior. We can set up guidelines like keeping our phones out of our bedrooms or our clothes on. Things like that can be wise, and you'll find ideas along those lines later in this book—but we need to be aware before we start that even our best intentions often fail. Adam and Eve probably thought they were extra smart and holy for saying, *Hey, let's make sure we don't even touch the tree! Then we can't eat the fruit.* But like them, in the face of something really enticing, our hearts are fickle, and our good intentions fizzle. (And if they don't, they can make us arrogant—another way of trusting ourselves more than our Creator.) We think our own happiness has the highest value and our own perception is the most trustworthy. This wreaks havoc in our lives and relationships, just as it did for Adam and Eve.

What Adam and Eve needed wasn't extra rules, better boundaries, or more willpower. They, like us, needed something far greater: a Rescuer.

They needed hope that there could someday be joy and freedom again: that the brokenness wasn't permanent and death wasn't the end of the story. They needed someone to pave a way back to the garden, to make things right between them and the God they had failed to honor.

Thankfully, God already had a rescue plan.

FOR REFLECTION

"NONE OF US HAVE ESCAPED UNSCATHED FROM SIN'S
DESTRUCTION. EVERYTHING WE TOUCH IS NOW DAMAGED IN
SOME WAY."

- WHERE DO YOU SEE OR EXPERIENCE THE WORLD BEING
  BROKEN?

- WHERE DO YOU EXPERIENCE BROKENNESS IN YOUR OWN
  BODY OR DESIRES?

"WE, LIKE ADAM AND EVE, FREQUENTLY QUESTION, 'DID
GOD REALLY SAY...?'"

- WHAT COMMANDS OF GOD ARE YOU MOST TEMPTED TO
  REASON YOUR WAY OUT OF?

- WHAT MIGHT YOU BE WORSHIPING OR TRUSTING (THAT ISN'T
  GOD) WHEN YOU ASK THIS QUESTION?

An Ultimate Hero

THE SAVIOR WHO BROUGHT COMPASSION AND REDEMPTION

EVER SINCE ADAM AND EVE left the garden, God's good design for sex has been muddied—and even used for evil and hurt. Not only do we feel the brokenness of our sexuality, but it's been used as a weapon for abuse. Not only is our experience of gender complicated by the fall, but people have used it as a tool for oppression and division. People have taken the image of God, which he created in us, and run it through the mud, and as a result people call God evil and blame all sorts of things on him. We might wonder if God is aware of the amount of pain that has come about in the area of sexuality.

Yes, he knows. And it grieves him deeply.

But the story isn't over.

Jesus was God's answer for the brokenness of everything, the mess that sin had caused. He came to make things right, to restore God's created design. He came to reunite an unfaithful bride (God's people) with her faithful husband (God). He came to show us the way to eternal life and to make it possible for us to be holy and whole, including in our sexuality.

But he came in a way no one expected.

He didn't come as a conquering king, a flying superhero, or a know-it-all untouched by the chaos around him. He came as a *human*. He came as a suffering servant.

And he came to die.

THE GOD WHO SUFFERED

I know life is complicated, messy, and often hard. Sometimes Jesus seems pretty fuzzy and hard to relate to real life. I mean, how much could a 1st-century Jewish rabbi really be able to relate to our world of Instagram, homework, cyber bullying, sports, makeup, friend drama, and queer theory?

He actually understands it much more fully than we do. Not *just* because he is all-knowing but because he's walked in our shoes (even if they were leather sandals). Jesus lived in our world—and yes, it was a different time period, but the essentials were the same. Jesus knows all about being "stuck" in a body with limits that didn't reflect his full nature. He, the eternal, uncontained God of the universe, took on a body that was bounded by space and time, felt pain and hunger, ached, bled, and died. He experienced teasing and rejection, loneliness and misunderstanding, temptation, injustice, and torture. He did this because of how much he loves us.

Jesus knew that our sins had us stuck—that we were incapable of choosing only good all the time. We couldn't make our way back to paradise with God any more than we could hike our way to the moon. The death, pain, and dysfunction that came as a result of the fall still shaped every part of our lives, and we couldn't shake it. We were like Hosea's wife, endlessly unfaithful to the God who loved us.

Hosea had to pay a price in money to win his wife back after her unfaithfulness. Jesus went one better. Out of his relentless, passionate, joyful love for us, he willingly went to the cross and died, breaking sin's curse so that if we trust in him, we won't have to die for our sins (Romans 6:23). He took the full weight of sin's punishment so that we could be free from it. He was faithful to us even when we had turned away, and he invited us into intimacy with him even when we'd done nothing to show him love. He experienced rejection and abandonment so that we could know the welcome of God. He was killed so that we could be given life.

Of course, the Creator of life could not stay dead! Jesus rose from the grave in the greatest possible victory. Evil did not have the last word. Even death had been defeated. And so there arrived a new kind of hope. It's a certain hope that, when we trust in Jesus, the struggles and longings we experience will not be permanent—and are not wasted. Jesus can heal your past scars, forgive your past sins, and invite you into a future that is free from shame and full of joy.

Remember that quote from Ephesians 5 that we saw in chapter 1? "'Therefore a man shall leave his father and mother and hold fast to his wife, and the two shall become one flesh.' This mystery is profound, and I am saying that it refers to Christ and the church" (5:31-32). Ultimately, Jesus died and rose again to unite his followers with him. This is the true intimacy that the Bible's picture of sexuality was always looking forward to.

And this has profound implications for our own sexuality today.

FRIEND OF SINNERS

But before we go on, I want to pause for a moment. Because you might be wondering whether the forgiving attitude toward sinners that I've just described *really* applies to sexual sins. Sometimes the church seems to treat sexual sin as the very worst of all—next to murder, perhaps. Maybe you've felt that personally. Perhaps you've come to expect judgment from Christians, not compassion or forgiveness. Maybe you feel like you can't discuss your struggles with porn at church. Maybe you suspect that Jesus doesn't have much compassion for gay people, or people who have slept with their boyfriend/girlfriend, or people who question their gender.

The opposite is true! And we're going to get into the details of particular situations and experiences in the following chapters (as well as considering what is and isn't sinful, and why)—but for now I want to show you one example of how Jesus actually responded to someone living in sexual sin. You can find it in John chapter 4.

Jesus is traveling through a place called Samaria. His disciples go into town to buy food, and Jesus sits down by a well to rest. Soon a Samaritan woman (with quite a reputation) comes to the well for water, and Jesus asks her for a drink—already breaking an unwritten rule about Jewish men not associating with Samaritan women. She responds in surprise, and Jesus answers:

> *"If you knew the gift of God, and who it is that is saying to you, 'Give me a drink,' you would have asked him, and he would have given you living water." (John 4:10)*

Jesus can give "living water"? It's an intriguing, if unexpected, invitation, but she's (of course) skeptical.

She logically points out that he has nothing to draw water with. Where is he going to get this "living water"?

Jesus answers by explaining what he meant in the first place.

> "Whoever drinks of the water that I will give him
> will never be thirsty again. The water that I will
> give him will become in him a spring of water
> welling up to eternal life." (v 14)

This sounds like a deal too good to pass up! "Sir," the woman responds, "give me this water, so that I will not be thirsty or have to come here to draw water" (v 15).

But here Jesus responds in another surprising way. "Go, call your husband, and come here" (v 16).

"I have no husband," she replies.

Jesus says:

> "You are right in saying, 'I have no husband'; for
> you have had five husbands, and the one you now
> have is not your husband. What you have said is
> true." (v 17-18)

Jesus had just brought up the woman's deepest shame and greatest place of pain, her source of insecurity—the thing that made her an outcast in her village. In that culture, going through divorce was not just a trauma but a disgrace, and one that left you in a very vulnerable position. Women didn't have the right to divorce their husbands, so this woman must have been abandoned five times (unless any of her husbands had died). We don't know the full backstory, but we can imagine how hurt and ashamed she was. She was considered soiled goods. Who would want her? Apparently one man, but not enough to marry her (which would have included provision and belonging); no, he just wanted to use her for his pleasure, and she was desperate enough to comply. Talk about sexually broken.

Jesus saw all of this when he looked at her. He knew her past, her present situation, her fears, and her shame without her telling him any of it. He didn't condone her sin, but he loved her. He knew that she was thirsty—thirsty for security, for safety, for real love. And Jesus knew that it was in himself that she would find what would truly satisfy her longings. That's what he meant by "living water."

The woman left her water jar and ran back to the village, calling to everyone, "Come, see a man who told me all that I ever did. Can this be the Christ?" (v 29). Because of her testimony, many Samaritans came to believe that Jesus was the Rescuer they'd been waiting for.

And so she became one of the first evangelists.

All because Jesus brought up the broken pieces of her past and gently held them up. He wanted her to know she didn't need to hide or fake it. She was loved and cared for as she was. And she was invited to a new relationship that was going to transform her life.

The point is, none of us need to be afraid to come to Jesus. He's not put off by your gender dysphoria, your compromised sexuality, your past abuse, your present temptations. He knows it all. Even though sin grieves him, Jesus loves you deeply and wants something more for you. Something found only in him.

THE END OF THE STORY

Jesus' death and resurrection invite us into a new life with him. We can know God personally and see our lives transformed to be like Christ. But even this is not the end of the story. It gets better. For now we're still fighting our sin, still aware of its impact in our lives, still facing struggles and disappointments and pain. But one day, if we're trusting in Jesus, all of that will be taken away completely.

When I was a kid and thought about heaven, I pictured sitting in the clouds or walking golden streets, doing a lot of singing. It seemed a lot better than the alternative (torment forever apart from God—see 2 Thessalonians 1:8-9), but it wasn't really what I otherwise dreamed of. Maybe you've felt the same way. My kids talk about heaven and ask me if they'll have hundreds of Lego sets and puppies and never have to go to bed (their ideal world). I've learned to say, "Either that or something way better!" It's a good reminder for all of us, I think. Maybe we hope heaven is a place where we'll see our loved ones again, or not have to work—where the weather will be perfect and we can do the things we most enjoy. But maybe all of that is just Lego sets compared to what Jesus is preparing.

> **"ALL OF THAT IS JUST LEGO SETS COMPARED TO THE ETERNITY JESUS IS PREPARING."**

The last book of the Bible describes eternity as the marriage supper of the Lamb (meaning Jesus—see Revelation 19:9). It's when Christ and his bride, the church (by which I mean all believers ever), are finally united in the ultimate way—without sin and doubt and fickle hearts and broken dreams. There's so much we don't know about what it will be like, but we do know that our bodies will be resurrected in perfection (1 Corinthians 15:35-55), we will be with God, and he will wipe away every tear from our eyes. There will be no more death or mourning or crying or pain (Revelation 21:3-4).

I certainly can't imagine it or paint you any kind of accurate picture. But I can promise you this: the worst that you've experienced in this life will be healed. There is no pain, grief, abuse, sin, or other scar that the Savior is not able to repair and redeem. And the *best* of all you've experienced in this life is just a faint shadow of the good that's coming. That includes sex—as well as the most beautiful beach at sunset, the thrill of skiing down a hill, your closest friend, and the taste of chocolate cheesecake. The best things this world has to offer are good gifts of its Creator, but they are nothing compared to the pleasures of eternity with Jesus. And he himself—the Redeemer and Bridegroom of every believer—will be the best part.

Friends, *that* is what's worth waiting for! That should stir us to turn away from the good-but-insufficient things that tempt us away from Christ. It will motivate us when life gets hard and the way of following Jesus looks like taking up a cross and dying. Life may have trouble, and following Jesus may be costly, but there is resurrection at the end. And the joy of eternity with our good God is more delightful than anything we can imagine.

YES TO JESUS

So the Bible starts and ends with a marriage: Adam and Eve, and Christ and the church. The interlude between is where we live. Even in this in-between, God wants to write a beautiful story in our lives—a story that reflects the bigger story of the gospel. He invites us to start that relationship now.

Thankfully, we don't have to earn anything of what Jesus offers (which is good, because we can't). But we do have to accept it. He will never force us; he simply invites. We have the choice to say yes to his proposal and be a part of the ultimate wedding that is yet to come. Or we can say no and choose life without Jesus... and therefore without the love he offers, the forgiveness for our sins, the new family he invites us into, and the home he is preparing.

There's a reason our relationship with Christ is compared to a marriage. Saying yes to Jesus means committing to him—to going where he goes, to trusting his promises, to loving him above all and forsaking anything that attempts to draw away our allegiance and affection. But even in this, we can rely on his grace and power for what we can't do on our own. The Bible is full of descriptions of what theologians call our "union with Christ." We are united to Jesus like a wife is united with her husband (Ephesians 5:29-30). He promises to never leave or forsake us (Hebrews 13:5). He sends his Spirit to dwell in us and give us life, helping us to know God and to fight sin (Romans 8:9-10; 1 Corinthians 2:12-13).

The point is, this intimate relationship with our Creator Bridegroom is not just something waiting for you in eternity if you're good. It's a relationship you are invited into *now* (John 17:3). Saying yes to Jesus begins an entirely new way of life, full of a new purpose and a greater hope, and it shapes everything about our life on earth—including our sexuality.

In the coming chapters, we're going to dig into some big topics around attraction, identity, and relationships. I'm hoping it will be practically helpful and encouraging to you. But the foundation for everything is the story of the gospel—the way we are created for relationship with God, the way sin brought destruction, and the way Jesus offers to redeem it all. How we think about pronouns, how we treat our significant other, the apps we use... all of it has to be shaped by this central relationship of our lives. There's not an inch of life that Jesus doesn't want us to bring to him. And whatever thirsts we bring, he will satisfy abundantly.

FOR REFLECTION

"ULTIMATELY, JESUS DIED AND ROSE AGAIN TO UNITE HIS
FOLLOWERS WITH HIM. THIS IS THE TRUE INTIMACY THAT
THE BIBLE'S PICTURE OF SEXUALITY WAS ALWAYS LOOKING
FORWARD TO."

- HOW IS JESUS THE PERFECT BRIDEGROOM?

- HOW CONFIDENT ARE YOU THAT HE CAN BE A BETTER SOUL-
  PARTNER THAN ANY HUMAN BEING COULD?

"SAYING YES TO JESUS BEGINS AN ENTIRELY NEW WAY OF
LIFE, FULL OF A NEW PURPOSE AND A GREATER HOPE, AND
IT SHAPES EVERYTHING ABOUT OUR LIFE ON EARTH."

- HAVE YOU SAID YES TO JESUS?

- IF SO, HOW HAVE YOU EXPERIENCED HIS LOVE AND
  TRANSFORMATION?

- IF NOT, WHAT ARE YOU STILL WAITING TO BE CONVINCED OF?

- FEEL FREE TO PRAY AND TELL HIM WHAT YOU'RE NOT SURE
  ABOUT!

WHY DOES GOD CARE WHAT I DO WITH MY BODY (IF I'M NOT HURTING ANYONE)?

BEING STUCK IN A BODY can be a drag.

My kids are always pretending they can fly, or read minds, or instantly transport themselves somewhere else. They're constantly dreaming up inventions to overcome the basic obstacles of time and space, which our bodies just can't seem to get around.

We may chuckle, but we're not that different. We bemoan the fact that our bodies are subject to acne and weight gain and bad hair days and stuffy noses and broken ankles... and (lucky for you) puberty changes that often come in awkwardly and at frustrating times. ("Did my voice have to crack while I was talking to her?" Or "Why did I wear white shorts today?")

Most of us have at least fleeting moments of wishing for someone else's body—or just to be out of our own. For some of us, the feelings can be almost crushing—a constant, nagging discomfort with our very gender, or an all-consuming sense of feeling ugly and unlovable. We may know God is good, but we don't always feel that way about everything he does. And we definitely don't always *feel* that way about our bodies.

And for good reason, right? Our bodies are imperfect, for sure. Most of us don't have supermodel looks or superhero strength; frequently our bodies get sick or hurt. Some of us are born with disabilities or chronic diseases that are a constant reminder that our bodies, along with the rest of creation, are broken and subject to frustration (Romans 8:20).

And to make matters worse, it can sometimes seem like God wants to make life in a body even harder for us than it was already. It might feel like the world around you knows how to really celebrate and enjoy sexuality, while Christians are buttoned-up and old-fashioned. It can seem like God is out to spoil our fun. That he *wants* us to feel bad about our bodies—he wants us to feel ashamed, inhibited, and embarrassed.

Nothing could be further from the truth. From God's perspective, humans—including our bodies—are the pinnacle of his creative work. We are a masterpiece of design, made in his own image and meant for a glorious purpose. Our bodies are his gift. That's why he cares so much about what we do with them. He made them, he knows what's best for them, and he has a bigger purpose for them.

Maybe you come to this chapter full of questions about why God had to give you the body you have. Or maybe you're asking why God can't just leave you to get on with using your body the way you want. Either way, we need to examine the story that God is writing through our bodies and see if what God has to say really is good news.

IS THE BODY BAD?

The first thing to be clear on is that our bodies are not separate from our "real selves." Sometimes we tend to think that our hearts are spiritual and our bodies aren't, or even that we are basically good but our bodies can be bad. After all, it's our eyes that cause us to lust, right? Sometimes our mouth seems to spit out angry words before we've even had a chance to think about them. My four-year-old, after punching his sister, told me, "I didn't want to do it, but my brain made me." It often feels like there's a "real me" deep inside that's good and trying to do the right thing, but my body and brain just won't cooperate!

A quick (mis)reading of Scripture seems to confirm this thinking. Galatians 5:16-17 says:

> *"So I say, walk by the Spirit, and you will not gratify the desires of the flesh. For the flesh desires what is contrary to the Spirit, and the Spirit what is contrary to the flesh." (NIV)*

In the past, some people took this to mean that the physical world (including the body) was evil, but the inner spiritual world (the "real you") was good, and so you had to discipline the body and treat it harshly to save your soul. Misunderstandings of the Bible have led some Christian traditions throughout history to be hard on the body and on sex in particular. But body-shaming is not a reflection of God's heart! Galatians 5 isn't talking about our physical bodies versus our inner soul. It's talking about our sinful nature—the part of ourselves that is prone to rebellion against God—and how those desires are at odds with the Spirit of God.

That wrong belief is still around today, showing up in new ways. "Have sex with whoever you want, as long as you love each other" (i.e. the heart matters and the body doesn't). "If you were born with a female body but you feel like a guy, embrace the real you" (i.e. your body lies but your mind tells the truth). "Yeah, I blew it, but I meant well" (i.e. my intentions are a better reflection of who I am than my actions). "God cares about the state of my heart" (i.e. he doesn't care about the state of my body).

This isn't the reality that God teaches about us as embodied people. So let's dig into a few key truths from Scripture about our bodies.

YOUR BODY IS YOU

The first two chapters of Genesis tell us how God created the world—a brilliant masterpiece of his creativity, wisdom, and love. But the crown of his creation is clearly humanity. Unlike pandas (though they're adorable), mountains lakes (though they're majestic), or cocoa beans (though they're delightful), God declared that *people* were made in his image (Genesis 1:27). In God's design, humanity bears a unique likeness to our Creator—and thus, a unique purpose and calling. We are like God—certainly not fully, as none of us can create worlds from nothing or know the thoughts of everyone before they think them. But somehow, in a compelling way, we are like him. We are meant to reflect elements of who he is and to be his representatives in the world.

Like God (and unlike the rest of creation), we are spiritual beings as well as physical. We can love intimately, design creative technology, choose good over evil, use language, and write books. But that's not all we are. When God created and defined us as people, he declared us not only to be made in his image but to be made male and female. He was talking about our physical design.

We are not people "stuck in" bodies, as if the "real us" is spiritual and the body is just some kind of tool we use or home we live in. No, listen to the description of God creating Adam:

> *"Then the Lord God formed the man of dust*
> *from the ground and breathed into his nostrils*
> *the breath of life, and the man became a living*
> *creature." (Genesis 2:7)*

God formed a man from dust, which is impressive—but don't miss the fact that what he formed was a body. Then into this body he breathed the breath of life, and the first human came to life. God didn't create a spirit human and then think up something to put it in. He formed a body, Adam, and gave him life.

Your body *is* you, made incredibly in the image of God, who gives it life. Even when God makes all things new in eternity, every believer will still have a body. It will be transformed (Philippians 3:21) and redeemed (Romans 8:23)—no more limping or wincing or puking or dying— but it will be their body. So how we treat and use our bodies really does matter.

GOD'S HUMAN BODY

There's another piece of evidence that God really does care about our bodies: as Christians, we believe that our redemption came when God himself took on a human body.

This is such a familiar teaching for most of us that we've lost sight of how incredible it is. Why would the God of infinite, uncontained power and glory choose to become a *human*? Jesus left heaven for a body that could experience pain, weakness, and even death. And he didn't choose to come as the most handsome man ever, clothed as a glorious king or some kind of divine Superman. No, he came as an embryo in the womb of a peasant girl. He knew hunger, pain, rejection, and weariness. His body bled and was broken so ours could be healed and made whole. "He himself bore our sins *in his body* on the tree, that we might die to sin and live to righteousness. By his wounds you have been healed" (1 Peter 2:24, emphasis added). Sinners can be saved because our God took on a body.

Even after his resurrection, Jesus remains embodied. His body could still be seen and touched by his friends (John 20:27). It was new, remade, and indestructible—but still very much a body. Jesus' incarnation and resurrection dignify the God-made wonder of the human body.

If you ever find yourself hating your body, remember that Jesus died to save it. Your body is integral to who you are, and it's more precious to God than you can imagine.

JOINED WITH CHRIST

We can't split up our soul from our body any more than we can separate the egg and the flour out of a muffin. Because of this, what we do with one affects the other. When our heart is captured by something, it will pull our body with it, and when our body acts, our heart is drawn along, too. That's why taking a deep breath can calm your emotions, and worry can cause us to bite our nails until our fingers bleed.

How we use our bodies shapes our hearts. This is where sex comes into the conversation. If our soul and our body are so interconnected, then sex is not just a physical act but a spiritual one as well.

Check out what Paul writes in 1 Corinthians 6:13-20:

> *"The body is not meant for sexual immorality, but*
> *for the Lord, and the Lord for the body. And God*
> *raised the Lord and will also raise us up by his power.*
> *Do you not know that your bodies are members of*
> *Christ? Shall I then take the members of Christ and*
> *make them members of a prostitute? Never!*
>
> *"Or do you not know that he who is joined to a*
> *prostitute becomes one body with her? For, as it is*
> *written, 'The two will become one flesh.' But he who*
> *is joined to the Lord becomes one spirit with him.*
>
> *"Flee from sexual immorality. Every other sin*
> *a person commits is outside the body, but the*
> *sexually immoral person sins against his own body.*
> *Or do you not know that your body is a temple of*
> *the Holy Spirit within you, whom you have from*
> *God? You are not your own, for you were bought*
> *with a price. So glorify God in your body."*

Paul is addressing the claims of people who were saying
that they could do whatever they wanted with their
bodies—they were going to die anyhow. Paul, though, says
that a Christian's body is meant for the Lord and is going
to be resurrected. Even more than that, he says our bodies
are *members of Christ himself* and *temples of the Holy Spirit*.
Just let that sink in for a moment! When I think about my
body, I'm more likely to think about the knee that causes
me problems, my hair which doesn't look great today,
or the autoimmune disease that keeps me from eating
bread—in other words, the imperfections. But God says
that my body is sacred.

When we come to Jesus, we are united with him in a way
that's hard to even understand. But this union with Christ
is the most important thing about us if we are believers.

Our identity, our primary relationship, and our biggest purpose all center around being joined with Christ. It's the greatest gift we've been given and the union we should most want to protect and honor.

So, Paul says, should I take this body that is joined with Christ and has been made holy by him, and use it for sexual unfaithfulness? Never! It's completely unthinkable. Jesus is the perfection of holiness and faithfulness. And when we are joined to him, we're called to use our bodies in the same way.

"JESUS IS PERFECTION. AND WE ARE JOINED TO HIM."

Sex is a physical re-enactment of the promise a couple has made to commit themselves wholly to each other, faithfully, for life. And it's a picture of God's holy, faithful love for his people. Ripping sex out of that context and using it purely for pleasure, outside of a sacred, lifelong commitment, is trying to become "one" with a person that you have no right or obligation to. It's treating your body—and sexuality—as dispensable, insignificant. Scripture says that when a Christian treats sex flippantly, he or she sins against their own body—and thus, against the God who has purchased their body with his own and made it his temple.

At the same time, hatred of our body—trying to harm it, escape it, or redefine it—also belittles the sacredness of our design. Your body is God's creation and his temple. He calls us to care for our bodies, trust him with their design, and honor him with their actions.

Obviously, there's a lot more to be said about how we can honor God with our bodies. What does that mean for gender identity? Porn? Dating relationships? Don't worry;

we'll get to those topics and more in the coming chapters as we look at the practical ways in which Christian beliefs play out in real life.

WHOLE-SELF DEVOTION

For now, let me just say this. There are two pits you can fall into when you think about honoring God with your body. One, as we talked about, is to think the heart matters most and what you do with your body is inconsequential. That would be the person who sings worship songs with her hands in the air and prays beautiful, lengthy prayers on Sunday, but on Friday night can be found getting drunk and sleeping around. That's clearly not biblical—James says that faith without deeds is dead (James 2:26).

But the pit on the other side is to go through all the motions of obedience, but to do so out of fear or duty and without a real delight in following God. This is like the guy who has never kissed a girl, never looked at porn, and reads his Bible daily, but who does so because he likes feeling better than everyone else (or because he's afraid of what they would think if he screwed up). God said that the Israelites who did this had hearts that were far from him (Isaiah 29:13).

As we seek to honor God, let's remember that his plan involves our hearts *and* our bodies—even though both are weak and sinful. The eternal God took on a human body so that he could redeem us, body and soul, and enable us to love him with all that we are.

FOR REFLECTION

"SOMETIMES WE TEND TO THINK THAT OUR HEARTS ARE SPIRITUAL AND OUR BODIES AREN'T, OR EVEN THAT WE ARE BASICALLY GOOD BUT OUR BODIES CAN BE BAD."

- HAVE YOU EVER FELT THIS WAY? IN WHAT WAYS?

- HOW DID THIS CHAPTER INFLUENCE YOUR THINKING?

"YOUR BODY IS YOU, MADE INCREDIBLY IN THE IMAGE OF GOD, WHO GIVES IT LIFE."

- TAKE SOME TIME TO TELL GOD WHAT YOU LIKE AND DON'T LIKE ABOUT YOUR BODY.

- CAN YOU ALSO START TO EXPRESS TO HIM YOUR CONFIDENCE IN HIS WISE DESIGN FOR BODIES AND SEX, AND FOR YOUR BODY IN PARTICULAR?

Identity

HOW DO I FIGURE OUT WHAT REALLY MAKES ME ME?

"**I'M GAY. IT'S JUST WHO** I am. If you can't accept that, then you're rejecting me."

Maybe you've had a friend say that to you. (Or something similar, like "I'm queer" or "I'm bi.") Maybe you've said those words yourself as you tried to express to someone you love the importance of what you're experiencing.

It's normal in our culture today to talk about our sexuality not as what we *do* or *feel* but as *who we are*. In other words, we think about our sexual attractions or orientation in terms of identity.

Identity is important because how we answer the question "Who am I?" affects the direction of our lives—what we do as well as what we think and feel about ourselves. The reverse is true, too: what we think, feel, and do affects how we answer the question of who we are. All of that can get a bit complicated! So we need to move away from the sexual identity question for a moment and focus on a broader one: what does God have to say about who we are? The answer provides a powerful foundation for all other conversations around identity.

IDENTITY AS PROMISE

Identity, and names that describe it, is actually a pretty important part of the Bible's story.

Scripture is full of examples of God giving people a new identity—showing that he not only knows them better than they know themselves, but also that he has bigger and better plans for them than they have themselves.

Take Abram. God had promised to make this man's descendants into a great nation, but things didn't look good; Abram had no son and was getting old. Even so, God kept making the same promise—and on one of those occasions, he added the following:

> "No longer shall your name be called Abram,
> but your name shall be Abraham, for I have
> made you the father of a multitude of nations."
> (Genesis 17:5)

Abraham was not yet a "father of many" (which is what the name means). His promised son, Isaac, was not yet conceived. But this was the identity God gave. The gift of this identity was a promise of something sure to come. It was something God was going to transform Abraham into. And it would shape Abraham for the rest of his life—and his family for generations to come. "No longer shall your name be called Abram, but your name shall be Abraham." God was saying, *This is who you will be. It is what I am making you into. And I want you to embrace that identity now, even though you can't yet see its fulfillment.*

Abraham wasn't the only person given a new identity by God. Jacob was renamed Israel (which means "wrestles with God") because he struggled with God, and God wanted him to remember what he had learned from it (Genesis 32:28). Gideon was hiding from an enemy army he deeply feared when God showed up and addressed him as "mighty warrior" (Judges 6:12, NIV). Simon, probably the most likely among all Jesus' disciples to wind up with his foot in his mouth by saying or doing something impulsive, was renamed Peter, meaning "rock"; Jesus said that he would build his church on the rock of Peter's declaration of faith (Matthew 16:18).

The God who spoke light into the darkness is not done naming (and renaming) things. He knows us completely—even better than we know ourselves. Again and again in the Bible, we see him giving people a new identity and then transforming them into what he has called them to be—a father, a warrior, a rock. These people got identities that were bigger and better than they themselves would have dreamed of. Today, God speaks a new identity over everyone who follows him: "But you are a chosen people, a royal priesthood, a holy nation, God's special possession" (1 Peter 2:9, NIV). God wants to speak a new identity over you, too—and it's an identity you can trust.

IDENTITY AS GIFT

The problem is, we're usually too busy trying to figure out our identity for ourselves to listen to what God is speaking over us. It's true of adults, too, but perhaps it's never more true than in the teen years. You're trying to figure out what to do with your life, where you fit in, what sets you apart, and how you can make a difference.

Those are all important questions! How you answer them will shape the choices that you make about the direction of your life.

But usually, the answers that we come up with are partial—or superficial. "I'm an athlete" or "I'm weird and awkward" or "I'm pretty" or "I'm fat" may be true (or may not be true, because sometimes our perception is flawed), but they're simply descriptors. They do not define our identity. And that's a good thing, because they can also be fragile.

For instance, I tend to find my identity in being a great wife, or a great writer, or someone who knows their Bible well. But inevitably something happens that reveals I'm not as great at any one of those things as I thought I was. When I fail to live up to one of those identities, it can feel crushing. I'm a bit of a perfectionist, and finding out that I was wrong about something (or, worse, that I wronged someone else) can feel like a giant wave has shipwrecked my sense of identity.

Maybe you've felt that same sense of unease. You took pride in being the best athlete and then broke your ankle; or you loved being known as the smartest kid in middle school, and then high school introduced you to students who knew much more. Maybe you found your security in good looks and then lost your hair to cancer; or your identity was wrapped up in your friend group, and they deserted you. Some people find their identity in their job or in their family and then find that even those aren't guaranteed to last. None of those things are sturdy enough to build an identity on.

Maybe that's why we're drawn to making our sexuality our identity. It feels less shaky than those other things. Our sexual attractions or gender identity can feel like a core, unchanging part of who we are, even more than being sporty or clever or awkward. It feels like we could build an identity on that.

But the truth is, it's still shaky. Preferences and attractions *do* sometimes change. Even some psychologists who don't believe in God are beginning to recognize that sexual and romantic attractions are more fluid than we've thought, and few people exclusively experience *only* gay or straight desires, making sexual identities harder to define and defend.[3] And the definition of gender gets pretty slippery once you exclude anything about the body.

It's helpful to understand your tendencies and desires because then you're better able to make informed choices. It's ok to acknowledge that the attractions you experience (and didn't choose) are to the same sex, or are to a confusing mix of people. It's ok to admit that you don't feel at home in the gender of your body. Attraction and feelings are real and important. But they are not the source of our identity. Your desires and your past don't own you, and they don't have to define you. Whatever you were, whatever you've done, whatever temptations pull at your heart... in Christ, you are a new creation (2 Corinthians 5:17).

> "YOUR DESIRES AND YOUR PAST DON'T OWN YOU, AND THEY DON'T HAVE TO DEFINE YOU."

Once again, what Jesus has to offer really is good news. He doesn't ask us to build (or figure out) our own identities. According to the Bible, our identity is a gift. Our gender is a gift. Marriage is a gift—and so is singleness. Our family is a gift. Our body is a gift. Our strengths and talents and personality and interests are gifts. And, if we are believers, the way God transforms us into the new identity he gives us is a gift. These gifts are all undeserved, yet freely given. And because God knows us better than we know ourselves—and he is always good—we can trust him with these gifts and learn to accept them with gratitude.

THREE LAYERS OF IDENTITY

I can almost hear the next question you're asking, though. *So, if God has spoken an identity over me... what is it?* Perhaps it's helpful to think about our identity in three layers.

The first layer is the way God has created you. You are created by God and in his image (Genesis 1:27; Ephesians 2:10). You were carefully designed long before your birth (Psalm 139:13). God has given you a certain body, certain family relationships and situations, certain characteristics. You can observe those things and choose to accept them as gifts (even if they're not what you might have chosen).

But the second layer, if you're a believer, is the way God has re-created you. Anyone who is in Christ is a new creation (2 Corinthians 5:17). You are chosen (Ephesians 1:4). You are beloved (Ephesians 5:1). You are forgiven (Colossians 1:14). You were bought at a price (1 Corinthians 6:20) and reclaimed for God (1 Peter 2:9-10). You are a member of his body (1 Corinthians 12:27) and his bride (Revelation 19:7-8). He calls you his friend (John 15:15). He has good works that he planned for you to do before the world was made (Ephesians 2:10). You are more than a conqueror through him who loves you (Romans 8:37). Just as when God renamed Abraham or Peter, this new identity that he speaks over us is unshakable and much more profound than any identities we speak over ourselves.

The third layer of our identity, in Christ, is the particular gifts and callings that he gives specifically to each of us as individuals. The Bible is clear that when we are in Christ, his Spirit lives in us and empowers us, both for holy living and for specific abilities which he gives us in order to make a difference in his kingdom. You have something unique to offer! But it's not your responsibility to conjure it up. It's simply to be faithful in finding ways to serve others with the skills and gifts God has entrusted to you. (Check out Romans 12:4-8 if you want to explore more of what this might look like for you.)

Friends, these layers of gifts are the identity God wants to speak over you! This identity does not depend on your sexual desires, your choices, or your feelings. It depends only on whether or not you belong to Christ—whether you accept his gifts. It's true (and important) that God does intend to do a work in your life that will transform your desires, your feelings, and your choices. But the starting point is simply coming to God as you are.

UNWRAPPING THE GIFT

Part of following Jesus is letting him define you. It's accepting what he says about you as true. It's receiving the gift he's given you. It's unwrapping it, figuring out how to use it, and learning to thank him for it.

For some of us, this is easy. You may be thankful for the body he's given you, for your sexuality, for your singleness in this season, for your salvation, and for the hope you have for this life and the next. Gratitude may flow easily.

But I'm certain it's much harder for others of us. Perhaps every outfit you try on is painful; every glimpse in a mirror makes it hard to be grateful. Maybe hearing your own name and pronouns spoken over you feels traumatic because you feel dissonance between that and your inward sense of identity. Maybe you didn't want the identity of gay or bi or trans, but your feelings seem like such an all-consuming part of you that trying to think of yourself in any other terms seems impossible. Or maybe you're proud of the identity you've chosen, whatever it is, and it seems unlikely that giving it up and accepting whatever God is giving you could possibly be better.

We all come at this from a different place; but we all ultimately wind up with a gift of identity from our Creator (written in our bodies and in his word), and we all have to determine what we will do with it. Can you accept that the identity God speaks over you is good? Can you trust that he made your body good? That his commands are for your good? That he loves you as you are? That he is sufficient for your deepest desires? And that he truly does have better plans for you than you have for yourself?

Just as God spoke a new identity over Abraham and then took him on a journey he never expected, so God wants to do a transforming work in *your* life. It may mean using the skills and talents he has given you in a way you don't expect, like my colleague Wes, who gave up a great-paying job to go into full-time ministry. Or Mark, who left full-time ministry and followed God's call to serve the local school as a custodian. It might mean that God will help you to live his way even when you are deeply tempted not to, like Christopher, who left his gay lifestyle for faithful singleness in response to Christ, or Jackie, who switched from wearing men's boxers back to women's underwear as an unseen "daily ritual of repentance."[4]

Accepting God's identity for us instead of figuring it out on our own isn't always easy. Jesus said, "If anyone would come after me, let him deny himself and take up his cross daily and follow me" (Luke 9:23). But it is always good, because God knows us better than we know ourselves, and he has plans for us that are better than we can imagine.

WHO KNOWS US BEST

God, after all, sees things more clearly than we do—we who have deceitful hearts, mixed motives, and limited perspectives. What we believe to be true about ourselves is not always accurate. Because of this, accepting what someone says about themselves as unquestionably true isn't always the most loving thing.

What if you had a friend with anorexia who saw herself as horribly fat, but you could see that she was becoming dangerously frail? Would you affirm her in her beliefs or tell her, in tears, what's true about her body despite her very real feelings? Or what if you had a friend who battled depression and felt they were worthless? Our feelings and views of who we are can be incredibly deep and persistent, but *that doesn't necessarily make them true.*

Just as real love may not mean accepting what a friend believes about their weight or their value, it may not mean accepting everything they say about their gender or sexual identity. But it *will* mean loving them the way they are, whether or not they see eye to eye with you. It will mean listening to their stories and struggles, even when those are messy and uncomfortable. It will mean wanting the best for them—perhaps not what *you* think is best or *they* think is best, but what God (the one who truly knows best) wants for them. And it will mean trusting that what God gives us—in our bodies, our names, and our callings—is better than any identity we could create for ourselves.

FOR REFLECTION

"SCRIPTURE IS FULL OF EXAMPLES OF GOD GIVING PEOPLE A NEW IDENTITY—SHOWING THAT HE NOT ONLY KNOWS THEM BETTER THAN THEY KNOW THEMSELVES, BUT ALSO THAT HE HAS BIGGER AND BETTER PLANS FOR THEM THAN THEY HAVE THEMSELVES."

- HOW DOES IT MAKE YOU FEEL TO HEAR THAT GOD KNOWS YOU BETTER THAN YOU KNOW YOURSELF?

- WHAT PARTS OF YOUR IDENTITY ARE HARDEST TO LET GO OF AND ALLOW GOD TO DEFINE?

"PART OF FOLLOWING JESUS IS LETTING HIM DEFINE YOU. IT'S ACCEPTING WHAT HE SAYS ABOUT YOU AS TRUE. IT'S RECEIVING THE GIFT HE'S GIVEN YOU. IT'S UNWRAPPING IT, FIGURING OUT HOW TO USE IT, AND LEARNING TO THANK HIM FOR IT."

- WHAT WOULD IT LOOK LIKE TO THANK GOD FOR HOW HE'S MADE YOU—EVEN IF YOU DON'T UNDERSTAND THE JOURNEY HE'S TAKING YOU ON, OR YOU FIND IT HARD TO SEE YOUR BODY AS GOOD?

- TRY TALKING WITH HIM ABOUT IT NOW.

Desire

WHAT AM I SUPPOSED TO DO WITH SUCH STRONG FEELINGS?

SHE CAME UP TO ME with her youth leader after I finished teaching a conference workshop, trembling and on the verge of tears. I could tell that I'd said something she didn't like. She looked down, shifting her feet. She told me she was a lesbian, then looked up at me and asked, "Doesn't God want me to be happy?"

My heart ached for her. I wished I could listen to her whole story and dig into the Bible together for a couple hours, rather than trying to formulate some kind of 60-second answer. I wanted to say *Yes! And no. It's not what you think. I see your tears; I hear your longings; I understand how hard all this sounds. You want happiness, and you think it's found in following your heart's desires. But God actually wants more for you, better for you, and it's found in giving those things up.*

But I knew that in two minutes' conversation, there was no way she would be convinced. And she had every right to be skeptical—it sounds completely backwards.

Sexual desire can be one of the strongest feelings we experience as humans. Falling in love not only captures our hearts but pulls on us in a very bodily way... and fills every moment of our thinking. This can be a thrilling time for a couple about to get married, but in your teen years it can set you up for a lot of heartbreak, distraction, and (sometimes) choices you'll regret.

Why would God make it so our desires are so strong when there's no godly outlet for them until marriage, which is likely many years down the road? And what about those who experience unchosen but consistent attractions to the same sex—does God expect them to just deny themselves these desires for life? Doesn't God want us to be happy?

FLASHES OF FIRE

To begin with, it's helpful to recognize that desire in itself is not positive or negative. It's part of being human, part of how God made us. What matters is the *object* of our desires and what we *do* with them. Sometimes we desire things that are of God—in line with his commands and the story he's writing. Other times we desire things that are against God's ways. The second kind, we should turn away from (more on that later). But the first kind, we should celebrate!

Did you know that there's a whole book of the Bible dedicated to the celebration of sexual love in marriage? It's called the Song of Solomon (or Song of Songs, in some translations). It's full of poetic, passionate expressions of desire between a husband and wife. It's traditionally been viewed as metaphorically about God's love for his people, which makes sense when we realize marriage is meant to be metaphorical! But it's clearly also human. If you read it, you're likely to be a little uncomfortable at the depth of emotion and longing shown at times. The bridegroom character says things like this:

> *"How beautiful and pleasant you are,*
> *O loved one, with all your delights!*
> *Your stature is like a palm tree,*
> *and your breasts are like its clusters.*
> *I say I will climb the palm tree*
> *and lay hold of its fruit.*
> *Oh may your breasts be like clusters of the vine,*
> *and the scent of your breath like apples,*
> *and your mouth like the best wine." (7:6-9)*

Are you blushing? I know those verses might feel a bit weird to read—the metaphors are a little lost on us culturally. But my point is, the Bible isn't embarrassed about our sexuality or the desires that go along with it. Within the boundaries of marriage, sexual desire is meant to be delighted in and celebrated.

The bride in the Song of Solomon is no less passionate, but as she declares her love and desire, she also has a message for the single young women around her:

> *"I adjure [urge] you, O daughters of Jerusalem,*
> *by the gazelles or the does of the field,*
> *that you not stir up or awaken love*
> *until it pleases." (2:7)*

Her call to not "stir up or awaken" these desires is repeated several times throughout the book. She seems to want her single friends to know *both* that sexual passion in marriage is beautiful and worth celebrating *and* that it's not to be aroused or invited before its time (marriage). For this lovesick couple, their desire is mutual, and they rightfully belong to each other (see 2:16). Their union is approved by God, and he wants to see them enjoy it to its fullest as it reminds them of something deeper and better: his love for them. The bride acknowledges this in 8:6 when she says:

> *"Set me as a seal upon your heart,*
> *as a seal upon your arm,*
> *for love is strong as death,*
> *jealousy is fierce as the grave.*
> *Its flashes are flashes of fire,*
> *the very flame of the Lord."*

The flashes of fierce love for each other—as strong as death, sealing them together—are of God. Their union is a picture of his love. Their desire is good. But she knows that for some of her friends, such desire would *not* be good because it's not the right object or the right time. It's the same for us as we are asked to submit not just our sexual activity but also our sexual desires to the rule of Christ.

IS MY DESIRE SIN?

We just saw that some desires are good to act on in certain circumstances, but not in others. There are also some desires which are never good to act on, in any circumstance. God created us to be people with desires, but in this fallen world where things are broken, not all our desires are good ones.

That's why, when I hear students say things like "It's just the way God made me" when they share about their sexual attractions or gender identity struggles, I have to disagree. God made you in his image, yes. But you're also broken and sinful, just like everyone else. Some of your desires—like the desire for sex outside marriage, or for a romantic relationship with a person of the same sex—are not of God, and they need to be resisted.

We need to start by recognizing that because we live in a fallen world, *all* of us face temptation. That means all of us experience being enticed by things that are not of God. These temptations may be fleeting or persistent; they may involve so-called "acceptable sins" or ones we feel we could never confess; they may be easy to resist or feel impossible to fight. But all of them are temptations toward sin.

Yet we don't need to feel guilty for temptations we didn't choose. We need to, instead, ask Jesus to deliver us from them and help us to live godly lives.

Same-sex-attracted pastor Sam Allberry explains:

> "Same-sex temptations (along with any other kind of temptation to sin) reflect our own fallenness. But this is not the same as saying **the presence of temptation** itself is a sin to be repented of. Scripture makes a distinction between temptation and sin ... we are to seek forgiveness for sin but deliverance from temptation." [5]

So, we don't need to beat ourselves up for the temptations that arise unbidden in our minds. But we do need to take ownership of what we do with them. If you experience same-sex attraction or gender dysphoria, or you wrestle with lust or any other temptation to sin, those struggles don't need to define you. They're not a reason for shame and hiding. They don't put you in a unique category of people who are hopelessly sinful. (News flash: that's all of us—or it would be, without the transforming work of Christ.)

What we *do* with these temptations, though, matters deeply. And I'm not just talking about what you do physically. Like I said, it's not just our sexual activity but also our desires themselves that need to be submitted to the rule of Christ.

As the apostle James puts it, we can get "lured and enticed" by our own desires (James 1:14). You keep on letting your attention drift to that girl's chest, or you let your sexual fantasies run and run inside your brain, or you tell yourself that since you experience same-sex attraction, God must have wanted it that way. This is sin. James 1:15 warns:

> *"Desire when it has conceived gives birth to sin, and sin when it is fully grown brings forth death."*

When we allow ungodly desires to "conceive" or take root—when we encourage and enjoy them, even if we're not acting on them physically yet—that's where sin comes in (see Matthew 5:28). And sin (but for the grace of God) will always have its end in death.

So, no, you don't need to be ashamed if you're being tempted to do something that you know is against God's word. But you do need to think seriously about how you're responding to that temptation. And that includes what happens in your mind and your heart as well as your body. God knows that too often what we think will bring happiness will really bring death. And he wants something much better for us—abundant life.

WHICH WAY WE'RE FACING

People talk about persistent sexual desires in terms of *orientation*. (And we'll talk about that more in chapter 10.) But the word orientation is about where we're facing, what we're focused on. Christ wants our hearts to be ultimately oriented toward him. When he is our focus, our aim, and our delight, our other desires begin to be reoriented, too.

A desire is fundamentally a search for satisfaction. Many of the things we desire don't really satisfy (like money, popularity, drugs, and yes, sex)—but Jesus does. Maybe you are looking for someone strong that you can depend on. The truth is, human strength always fails. But God is your all-powerful Protector and Defender. Or maybe your heart is drawn toward someone beautiful—but human beauty is imperfect and fading. Christ's beauty is limitless and awesome. Maybe you yearn to be seen, known, and treasured for who you are. Marriage is meant to do this, to a degree—but spouses

"IN THE END, DESIRE IS REALLY MEANT TO LEAD US TO JESUS."

still battle self-focus and get frustrated at each other. God is the only one who can understand every part of you completely and love you perfectly. Maybe you want someone who will always be there for you. People have limited capacities; they leave, and at some point they die. Jesus is the only one who will *always* be with you. He is the only one whose love can completely satisfy.

In the end, desire is really meant to lead us to Jesus, the only one who can fully fulfill us and give us the things we need and long for. This means that when we surrender our desires to him—thinking we are giving up something dear—we actually find something better on the other side. As C.S. Lewis famously said:

> *"It would seem that our Lord finds our desires not too strong, but too weak. We are half-hearted creatures, fooling about with drink and sex and ambition when infinite joy is offered us, like an ignorant child who wants to go on making mud*

> pies in a slum because he cannot imagine what is
> meant by the offer of a holiday at the sea. We are
> far too easily pleased." [6]

I don't know what it is exactly that you're "lured and
enticed" by, but I do know that Jesus is a better fulfillment
of your deepest longings than anything or anyone else
ever could be. And he wants to help you turn toward
him—and toward infinite joy.

A BATTLEGROUND AND A WINDOW

With all of that in mind, here are two useful ways to
think about temptation.

First, temptation is a battleground. It's a chance for us
to determine (and show) what has our primary allegiance,
our deepest desire. Scripture says, "Beloved, I urge you ...
to abstain from the passions of the flesh, which wage war
against your soul" (1 Peter 2:11). Our "natural" desires, if
they are against God's word, are attacking our soul, and
their end is death. So we need to fight them. Do we believe
that if we do without this temporary pleasure, we will find
God to be enough to satisfy our deeper longings? Do we
trust that what he is asking us to do is ultimately good?
And do we believe that his Spirit has power enough to
equip us to resist the temptation, no matter how strong?

Temptation is a battleground for worship, a test of faith.
But it's also an opportunity to build faith. Because every
time we deny our sinful desires and say yes to Jesus, he
shows himself to be faithful. We build spiritual "muscles"
of faith as we choose to follow God and find him to be
what he said he would be.

Second, temptation is also a window, in that it reveals
something about our hearts. Persistent temptations

expose our inner desires or fears. Jesus said, "The mouth speaks what the heart is full of" (Matthew 12:34, NIV). In other words, the things that take up residence in our hearts will show up in our thoughts, our words, and our actions. By paying careful attention to which temptations have a draw on us, we can observe what idols our souls may be drawn to and what lies our hearts might be believing. And we can bring them to Jesus for both forgiveness and transformation.

This is why simply stifling desires and pretending they aren't there rarely works and isn't really honoring God. We need Jesus to work on our hearts if we are to overcome temptation for the long haul. And this is something he is glad to do! Continually watching the state of our hearts and staying close to Jesus is the best strategy for fighting temptation. When we're walking closely with Jesus and our hearts are full of him, it's easier to see the lies that sinful desires try to make us believe. Whereas when we're discontented, proud, or self-focused, giving in to temptation becomes more and more attractive. That's why the Bible says:

> "Above all else, guard your heart, for everything you do flows from it." (Proverbs 4:23, NIV)

What specific desires most frequently pull at your heart and turn it away from Jesus? What lies is the enemy trying to convince you to believe? I encourage you to pause right here in order to pray. Offer these desires to God. Tell him what you want and how deeply it pulls on you. Confess the places you've gone to seek satisfaction apart from him. Ask him to reveal himself to you as capable of fully satisfying any good desire that lies at the heart of the temptation, and to give you strength to seek him in your longings.

A BALM OF HOPE

I want to say one final word to those of you who feel your desires as a heavy weight. Perhaps they're same-sex desires or struggles with lust; perhaps they're temptations toward compromise with your boyfriend or girlfriend. Please hear this: You are deeply loved by God. And while his call to holiness is a high standard, you're not asked to work it out on your own. If you are in Christ, his Spirit is in you, making you holy. And if you ask God for his help to fight sin, he gives it eagerly. Sometimes temptations can feel unbearably strong, but Jesus promises that he will not allow them to be more than you can bear; he will provide a way out (1 Corinthians 10:13). He might provide a way by removing the desire when you ask him, or by increasing your strength of desire for him, or by giving you a community that can help you stay strong. But he will certainly provide.

Some people find that, as they grow in faith and learn to lean on Jesus when they are tempted, desires like same-sex attraction become much easier to deal with—although the battle remains lifelong. For others, such desires go away completely. I don't know what story yours will be. But I do know that God is good, that he has good things for you, and that he is capable of transforming you—whatever desires you face.

Rachel Gilson, whose story includes wrestling with same-sex desires, writes this:

> "Faithful same-sex-attracted Christians bring to the church and to the world ... this clear path: a vision of Jesus more beautiful than romance, of the Spirit empowering us to live in holiness, and of the Bible not as a death sentence but a balm of hope." [7]

I know the girl who came up to me in tears felt in that moment like the words of the Bible were a death sentence. My prayer for her—and for you—is that you would come to see that they are really the very opposite.

FOR REFLECTION

THE CHAPTER TALKED ABOUT HOW TEMPTATION BECOMES TWO THINGS: A BATTLEGROUND AND A WINDOW.

- WHAT SPECIFIC TEMPTATIONS MOST FREQUENTLY PULL AT YOUR HEART?

- CAN YOU IDENTIFY THE DESIRE THAT IS AT THE ROOT OF THEM, AND HOW JESUS CAN SATISFY THAT DESIRE?

- WHAT LIES IS THE ENEMY TRYING TO CONVINCE YOU TO BELIEVE IN ORDER TO WIN THIS PARTICULAR BATTLE OVER YOUR HEART?

"WE ARE ASKED TO SUBMIT NOT JUST OUR SEXUAL ACTIVITY BUT ALSO OUR SEXUAL DESIRES TO THE RULE OF CHRIST."

- WHAT DESIRES MIGHT YOU NEED TO SUBMIT TO CHRIST, ASKING HIM EITHER TO TRANSFORM THEM OR TO EMPOWER YOU TO RESIST THEM?

- HOW DOES 1 CORINTHIANS 10:12-13 ENCOURAGE OR CHALLENGE YOU?

Gender

WHY DOES IT MATTER WHAT PRONOUNS I USE?

A FRIEND OF MINE POSTED on social media recently that anyone who tries to tell you what gender you can be clearly doesn't believe in freedom. Her mindset is reflective of our culture's. Be whoever you want to be, right? Can't we just leave people to choose whatever they want, if they're not hurting anyone?

That's a legitimate question—loaded with deep emotions, for some. But underneath it are some big assumptions about what gender is and why it matters. So, before we go any further, a brief note about the words we're using is important. (And if you skipped chapters 4-5 on the body and identity, please go and read those first, as they set an important foundation.)

DEFINING GENDER

The way people talk about gender has changed recently. When I was a teen, my friends and I treated the words *gender* and *sex* (as in biological sex) as pretty much interchangeable: they meant the same thing. Now many people see them not only as distinct but as disconnected—your gender may be different than your sex. This can result in confusion about how these terms are used, so let's see if we can bring some clarity.

Biological sex is straightforward (unless you're one of a small percentage of people born intersex, which we'll talk about more in a minute). Medically and scientifically, "an organism is male or female if it is structured to perform one of the respective roles in reproduction ... There is no other widely accepted biological classification for the sexes."[8] If you have XY chromosomes and male sex organs, you are male; your body is structured to reproduce by producing sperm. If you have XX chromosomes and female sex organs, you are female; your body is structured to reproduce by producing the egg (and sustaining the baby through pregnancy).

Gender, on the other hand, has become far from straightforward. It's generally accepted to mean "the psychological, social and cultural aspects of being male or female."[9] But people have also begun to say that your gender doesn't have to be the same as your biological sex—and doesn't even have to be split into just male and female. One website simply says, "Your gender identity is how you feel inside and how you express those feelings."[10] This definition is

"GOD SEES YOU, HE KNOWS IT ALL, AND HE LOVES YOU DEEPLY."

meant to be freeing, but it's also very vague. Feelings and cultures change! Without an attachment to anatomy, how can we even define a man or a woman? All we're left with is stereotypes.

I chose to call this chapter "Gender" and not "Sex," but I want to start by affirming that in the Bible, those two things aren't separate. From the beginning God created us as integrated people, male and female. Our bodies can't be disentangled from our spirits (as we saw in chapter 4). Gender, then, is not primarily about feelings and expectations; it's about created design. God created the two sexes as distinct, complementary, and purposeful. Whether God created you male or female, he's gifted you with that identity, and he wants you to live out your manhood or womanhood in a way that images your Creator and contributes to the world around you.

Let me be clear on about what I *don't* mean by that. I don't mean that if you're female, you have to be into fashion and baking, or that if you're male, you need to be athletic and assertive. I don't mean that your gender is only about marriage and reproduction. And I don't mean that if you have a deep sense of disconnection between your outward looks and inward feelings, those feelings don't matter. Whatever your emotions coming into this chapter, God sees you, he knows it all, and he loves you deeply. And he wants you to understand that your gender is his good gift.

FREEDOM AND BOUNDARIES

Some people are surprised to learn that the Bible doesn't tightly define the way gender is expressed. While there are some instructions on how men and women interact in marriage and in the church (see Ephesians 5:22-33; 1 Corinthians 11:2-16; 14:29-35; 1 Timothy 2:8-15; Titus 1:5-9; 1 Peter 3:1-7), there is an abundance of freedom in how men and women live out their gender. In fact, at times Scripture seems to highlight men and women who broke with cultural tradition (such as Deborah being the only judge of Israel portrayed in a fully positive light, or God choosing Jacob, who preferred staying home with his mother and cooking, over Esau the hunter).

In other words, as the respected authors Tim and Kathy Keller write, "Rigid cultural gender roles have no biblical warrant. Christians cannot make a scriptural case for masculine and feminine stereotypes."[11] The Bible is silent on who should do the cooking or the lawn-mowing, who should play sports or cry more. That means that each of us should be unafraid to bring all that God has made us to be, not try to fit into some stereotype.

Yet the Bible does *not* accept an erasing of gender distinctions. When cross-dressing or the blurring of gender is mentioned, it's prohibited (see Deuteronomy 22:5 and 1 Corinthians 11:3-16). We may instinctively resist boundaries; they feel stifling, limiting. *What if I don't want to be male? What if I don't feel like a girl? What if I don't fit either and don't want to be limited to two options?* But God wants us to honor the boundaries and distinctions he created as good. He wants us to embrace being the man or woman he has made us to be. Why? Because we gain something beautiful from the diversity and union of the sexes.

GENDER AND THE IMAGE OF GOD

Our culture talks about gender in terms of identity (which is to do with your inward feelings) and expression (which is how you want to be seen by others). Both of these are individualistic, me-focused ideas. But biblically, my gender is not just about me. It's a part of how I can reflect God.

Here's how our creation is described in the first chapter of Scripture:

> *"So God created man in his own image,*
> *in the image of God he created him;*
> *male and female he created them." (Genesis 1:27)*

Humanity is said to be made in God's image, male and female. This means our sexed bodies are a core part of our humanity and of how we reflect our Creator. Our sex isn't incidental, like the color of our eyes or the size of our feet. It's way more important than those things.

And the distinction between male and female goes far deeper than many of us realize. If you are male, you have XY coding in the DNA of *every single cell of your body*. And if you are female, you have XX coding everywhere—in your arteries, in your fingernails, in your eyes, in your lungs. So being male or female is about a lot more than just sex organs. It's embedded throughout your being—illustrating that God made us as whole, integrated people. Our gender, then, is part of how we image God.

Ok, you might be thinking, *but how?* I want to highlight two ways.

WE'RE FRUITFUL TOGETHER

We're all aware of the most evident place where gender shows up. The sexed bodies of a man and woman are not just clearly different, but they're obviously designed to be used together for reproduction. (I won't go into the details!) Incidentally, that's where the term gender came from; it has the same root as *generate*, *progeny*, and *genitals*, which all have to do with producing or giving birth.

Humans have the opportunity to bring new life into the world through sexual union. And that's a significant part of being made in God's image—after all, he's the one who created the world in the first place. Our sex is what gives us the potential to become co-creators with him and to fulfill his first command to "be fruitful and multiply and fill the earth" (Genesis 1:28).

I should add that becoming a parent is not the only way your gender can be life-giving. I know a single man who decided to be a father-figure to kids in North Minneapolis who were growing up without dads. An older woman unable to have children of her own made a significant impact in my husband's life when he was a child. You can be motherly or fatherly (or brotherly or sisterly) without ever having biological children. While this isn't the place to discuss exactly what makes a mother role different than a father role (it's complicated, and there isn't space), it's clear we all need people of the opposite sex in our lives, not only when we're little but later, too. The two genders are designed to come together to bring life.

Which leads me on to my next point.

WE HELP EACH OTHER

I used to wonder why God didn't create us asexual, like starfish. There wasn't any *need* to design two sexes—we could have reproduced by touching toes or something. Everything would be so much simpler if we were all the same!

But it wouldn't reflect (or glorify) God as much. You see, God—as Father, Son, and Holy Spirit—has always displayed unity in diversity. Being different—and working together within that—is a reflection of who he is. That's true in marriage and sexual intercourse, but it's also true in other, everyday spheres. Both sexes are unique, complementary, relational reflections of God. Each is just as valuable as the other, but they are deliberately designed to be different and to need each other.

We already discussed in chapter 1 the moment when God said, "It is not good that the man should be alone; I will make him a helper fit for him" (Genesis 2:18). God understood (designed, even) Adam's need for relationship, and he planned a way to meet it. Taking a rib from the side of the man, he sculpted a woman. She was Adam's custom-made match: "a helper fit for him." That word *fit* means "corresponding to" or "suitable for"—it means Eve was both *like* and *opposite to* Adam. Like two puzzle pieces that fit together—not exactly the same but not randomly different either—they were made perfectly fitted for each other.[12]

If all Adam had needed was companionship, God could have made him another man. They could have gotten along great. But he didn't, because Adam needed someone different from him. Or God could have given him a dog—man's best friend, who would follow him everywhere and always be excited to see him. But Adam needed someone more similar to himself than that. He needed someone *like* him and yet *unlike* him—in just the right ways.

And that was what would most clearly show off God's image.

You see, the word *helper* is not like *assistant* or *sidekick*. It's not a lesser role, just someone to take a bit of pressure off. The Hebrew word for helper, *ezer*, is most often used in the Bible to describe God, or else military strength brought in to win a battle. (For example, see Exodus 18:4; Deuteronomy 33:26, 29; Psalm 121:1-2.) It's strength in an area that desperately needs it. It's powerful.

Adam needed some serious help. He was not going to be able to follow God's call to fill the earth and subdue it, or to reflect God's image to the world around him, all on his own. Man and woman needed to work together.

MORE TO THE STORY

That's still true today. Churches, businesses, education, politics, and just about every other arena of life are better off with both men and women actively working in those spaces. God created gender distinctions so that we complement each other, contribute to society, and show off multifaceted aspects of his image in the world.

REAL LIFE CAN BE A MESS

It's one thing to read the creation story and see God's goodness in his design of men and women together bearing his image, creating new life, and taking care of his world. But it's quite another to think about the world we know. We see women treated as sex objects rather than valued as helpers. Guys are teased if they show emotion or are into fashion; girls are told they might inwardly be male if they love competitive sports and can't stand dresses. Most of us have experienced some kind of expectation to be different than we are. And some of us have dealt with this on a more intense level.

I have a friend with a female body who identifies as male; she* told me that she felt like she was walking around with her shoes on the wrong feet, constantly uncomfortable with her own gender and longing for her body to match who she felt she really was. I've known others who didn't necessarily want to switch genders but also weren't comfortable with being viewed as a girl and would rather be known as "they." I know men who say they would have identified as trans if they'd grown up in today's culture, because they never felt like they fit in with other guys.

---

*Throughout this book I'm using pronouns that match biological sex for the sake of clarity and leaving out some names for the sake of privacy. Some of the people mentioned go by different pronouns and some do not.

There are lots of reasons why people might feel this type of discomfort. It's normal for there to be a certain uneasiness with our bodies during puberty because, well, they're changing. It can be a lot to get used to. The gender stereotyping in our culture can add to the awkwardness if we don't fit the mold. Sometimes the discomfort is heightened because we've suffered abuse, bullying, or discrimination. Sometimes we see others experimenting with different queer identities, and they seem happier; we wonder if we would be, too. Sometimes the pressure feels innate, something that's been felt and suffered from the time we were small.

For a very small percentage of people, there's actually physical confusion. Intersex people may be born with a combination of male and female tissue or chromosomes. This can lead to pain and confusion, and it requires a lot of love from the people around them as they sort through it. But this isn't cause to question the goodness or clarity of God's created order. After all, intersex conditions are only one type of the innumerable differences or disorders that people can be born with. Even without any medical diagnoses, most of us will experience at some point a body that doesn't work how it should. Living in a broken world has made it normal to experience brokenness in our bodies, and we all feel that to differing degrees.[13]

Scripture doesn't discount any of this messiness. If anything, it offers understanding. Jesus himself both taught that God created two sexes *and* seems to have acknowledged that some people were born with sexual

> "SCRIPTURE DOESN'T DISCOUNT THIS MESSINESS. IT OFFERS UNDERSTANDING."

abnormalities that didn't quite fit the categories (Matthew 19:12). Sin brought a curse that affected everything, including our minds and bodies. Christians, with this knowledge, ought to sympathize best with those who struggle, to show the greatest compassion to the hurting, and to break down hostility and injustice wherever it shows up. We should be the first to love those who disagree, and the best at creating a community where all are valued. We should be quick to affirm that *all* people are made in God's image, deserving of love and dignity and incredibly valuable. But we can also affirm, like Jesus, that God's created design of male and female is good. It's not redefined by the messiness we experience in gender.

WHO I WAS MADE TO BE

What does all of this mean for you and me, practically speaking? Well, we've got to figure out what it looks like to embrace the gender God made us with, without falling into the trap of just basing our identity on a stereotype. I know that will feel pretty easy for some, but much more difficult for others.

Jackie Hill Perry tells the story of how she met Jesus as a lesbian "stud" who hid all signs of femininity. After trusting Christ, she felt convicted to buy clothes that reflected her God-given identity as female. Clothing might seem like a small thing, but Jackie knew it made a statement. She wrote about her shopping trip:

> *"It would be a declaration. A symbolic shout that the woman that once was lost now had been found ... Disrobing myself of clothing that projected an image unlike the one I was born as ... was an act of reminding myself of who I was made to be."* [14]

Who were *you* made to be? Jesus, the one who gave you your body, your identity, and your hormones, promises to give you life to the full in your following of him. He wants you to trust him—with your identity, your life, and yes, your gender.

But please don't journey alone! Remember, we're made to need each other. Find a community of people who love you and God's word, and who can walk with you as you discover who God made you to be—and how your gender can show off his image and be a blessing to the world.

EXTRA: PRONOUNS

One of the biggest questions surrounding gender is: what about pronouns? When you have a friend who wants to go by pronouns different from their created gender, what do you call them? It's one thing to have an abstract theological conversation about issues. But this trans person is made in the image of God, is deeply loved by him, and should be honored and loved by us as well. And most likely, someone embracing a trans identity is also dealing with significant emotional pain. Trans students have a significantly higher risk of suicide than their peers,[15] which just shows how important it is for them to have caring friends who stick by them, even if we don't understand or agree with all their decisions. I've heard too many stories of trans teens who felt abandoned by their church friends once they "came out." Whatever we think about pronouns, clothing, and surgeries, let's be loving friends who stick around!

There are differing views about pronouns among Christian leaders. Some people[16] think it's an act of hospitality to use the pronouns by which someone wants to be referred to. If we're not willing to show trans people the basic respect of calling them what they want to be called, we're probably closing the door to any real further relationship.

Others say it would violate their conscience to use a pronoun that doesn't align with someone's birth sex because it feels like a lie.[17] It risks undermining the importance of God's creation of our sexed bodies and of us as integrated people, body and spirit. And sometimes the most loving thing is to tell someone the truth.

There are people I respect who land on both sides of the pronoun debate.

Still others acknowledge that different situations may require different answers.[18] If someone comes to youth group dressed as a boy and says their name is Tom, it might be best to refer to them "he" and welcome them, rather than questioning them about their sex organs. That's very different from your best friend telling you she wants to go by male pronouns now, right?

While the Bible doesn't directly address pronoun usage, what's clear is that we need to be able to speak in truth and love (Ephesians 4:15). We want to welcome and love people just as they are (Romans 15:7) but be willing to boldly call them to follow Christ, which involves obedience whatever the cost (Luke 9:23). Before you jump to reasserting whatever opinion you had when you opened this book, I hope you think through the weighty implications on both sides and ask yourself questions like these:

- If you refer to your friend by their preferred pronouns, will it signal that you're affirming their decisions or just caring for them as a person? Will others who overhear understand or be misled? Will using these pronouns tempt you to embrace the world's perspective, or will you stay strong in your convictions as you show love?

- If you refer to your friend by the pronouns of their birth sex, will it signal a rejection of their friendship? Since they're likely to think so, how can you find ways to show increased care and love to them while holding to your beliefs?

As followers of Jesus, let's commit to being good friends to those whose who are wrestling through gender issues! Let's love them—unconditionally and joyfully—while ultimately pointing them to the goodness of Jesus and his ways.

FOR REFLECTION

"OUR SEXED BODIES ARE A CORE PART OF OUR HUMANITY
AND OF BEING MADE IN GOD'S IMAGE."

- HOW DO YOU FEEL READING THIS STATEMENT?

- HOW IS YOUR GENDER A REFLECTION OF GOD?

- HOW CAN IT BE LIFE-GIVING TO THE WORLD?

"MOST OF US HAVE EXPERIENCED SOME KIND OF
EXPECTATION TO BE DIFFERENT THAN WE ARE. AND SOME
OF US HAVE DEALT WITH THIS ON A MORE INTENSE LEVEL."

- HAVE YOU FELT ANY DISCOMFORT WITH YOUR GENDER?

- DO YOU TEND TO THINK OF YOUR FEELINGS IN GENERAL—
  ESPECIALLY STRONG FEELINGS—AS BEING THE WAY THINGS
  REALLY ARE, OR AS SOMETHING DISTINCT FROM THE WAY
  THINGS REALLY ARE?

- HOW WOULD EACH OF THESE VIEWPOINTS AFFECT THE WAY
  YOU LIVE?

Singleness

WHAT IF I NEVER GET MARRIED?

HAVE YOU EVER BEEN THE "third wheel" hanging around friends who all seem to have a date? Or had a well-meaning adult ask you why you're not dating someone? Even before you're old enough to be married, people around you often expect you to have a "special someone"—after all, who wants to be alone?

Singleness in our culture (and in the church) is sometimes treated as a lesser kind of status. It's assumed that you'd be married or dating if you could find the right person, but because you can't, you're stuck being alone. It's assumed that our sexuality needs to be expressed in having sex with someone. And so, when we ask people to reserve sex for marriage—and marriage for a man and a woman—people tend to think we're relegating singles and gay people to a lifetime of loneliness and lack. But God views singleness very differently.

Becket Cook is a man who loves to testify to this truth. He was living the ultimate life of freedom and indulgence, according to many, when he met Christ. He lived in LA, socialized with the elite, traveled the world, and enjoyed a gay lifestyle. Then he heard the good news of Jesus. He traded all of it for Christ, and now lives (joyfully) as a single person in love with Jesus. He says that people regularly ask him, "Isn't it unfair that you have to be alone for the rest of your life?" This is his response:

> *"I'm not alone. I am in a personal relationship with the King of the universe—the best and most exciting relationship I've ever been in! A relationship that makes all human relationships pale in comparison ... [Jesus] never cheats on me, he's always faithful, and he will never leave me or forsake me! (All that cannot be said about my ex-boyfriends.)"* [19]

How is it possible for Becket to talk like this? He's experienced intimacy with Jesus and knows it's better than anything else! And also, he understands singleness from God's perspective.

The Bible views singleness as a gift from God (see 1 Corinthians 7:7-9, 25-31), an opportunity to focus on God in an undivided way (1 Corinthians 7:32-35), and at times a better option than marriage (1 Corinthians 7:38-40; Matthew 19:10-12). Ultimately, Christian singleness, whether for a season of time or for life, honors Christ as the ultimate object of our love. And it's good!

WHAT YOU DON'T NEED TO CHANGE
The apostle Paul spends significant time in his first letter to the Corinthians teaching on marriage and singleness. He instructs husbands and wives to stay together and

share their bodies with each other. He instructs single people to stay single if they can do so in a way that is self-controlled and focused on God, but says that they're also free to marry. But the center of his argument is this general principle:

> *"Only let each person lead the life that the Lord has assigned to him, and to which God has called him ... In whatever condition each was called, there let him remain with God." (1 Corinthians 7:17, 24)*

Paul addresses slaves and free people, Jews and Gentiles, and married and single people, and his basic word of advice is: don't be preoccupied with changing your status in this life. You don't need to change your situation to honor God. You don't have to become Jewish. You don't have to get married (or divorced from an unbelieving spouse). You don't even have to find a way to free yourself if you're a slave (though if you can, go ahead). Why? Because ultimately our primary status, as believers, is that we have been bought with a price and are now servants of Christ (v 23). We have a new allegiance that overshadows any other status or relationship. What counts is being in Christ.

This may sound startling to us because we tend to put a lot of focus on our status and situation in life. If we're single, we can focus on finding the right person to date. If we're dating, we think about marriage. High-schoolers look forward to college life. College students think about the perfect career. An employee wishes for a job with more income and influence, while a boss wishes for a job with less stress. Maybe you think making the football team or the honor roll would make you happy.

But Paul wants to remind us of something incredibly important: this life—and all the situations that go with it—is temporary. And in perspective, it's *really* short. He wants to remind us that the end of this world is coming soon; this life is a drop in the bucket. Eternity, on the other hand, is, well, *forever*. Things like whether we had a girl to ask to prom, whether we made it on the dance team, or whether we earned a lot of money aren't going to matter when we get there. And even things like whether we're married or single—huge though they feel right now—are temporary! In heaven, Jesus says, we won't be married (Luke 20:35)—or rather, there will just be one marriage, that of the church to Christ.

Wherever you are in life, Paul says, you can honor God right there. You can honor God as a single person—or married. You can honor him at age 14—or at 98. You can honor him as a celebrity—or as a slave. You can honor him as a student, a janitor, a burger flipper, a soccer player, a friend. You don't need to wait until you're married (or have a degree, or a great job, or a social media platform) to make a difference in his kingdom. You don't need to worry too much about how long you'll be single. Regardless of what culture may tell us, your relationship status isn't the most important thing about you.

> "WHEREVER YOU ARE IN LIFE, YOU CAN HONOR GOD RIGHT THERE."

SINGLENESS IS GOOD

So that gives us one reason why Becket Cook could be so jubilant about being single: he recognized what was more important. Even so, you might be thinking, "I'd rather honor the Lord with a partner than alone!" But the

Bible actually tells us singleness is *good*... that it can even be better than marriage. That might seem surprising—after all, we spent a couple chapters talking about how marriage is a picture of God's love and a living metaphor of our relationship with Christ. Marriage is beautiful, important, deeply spiritual, and can be exceedingly good. But *so is singleness.*

Paul states, for example, that widows are free to marry whomever they wish, as long as it's someone who shares their faith, but he says, "Yet in my judgment she is *happier* if she remains as she is" (1 Corinthians 7:40, emphasis added). He also writes:

> "I want you to be free from anxieties. The unmarried man is anxious about the things of the Lord, how to please the Lord. But the married man is anxious about worldly things, how to please his wife, and his interests are divided. And the unmarried or betrothed woman is anxious about the things of the Lord, how to be holy in body and spirit. But the married woman is anxious about worldly things, how to please her husband.
>
> **"I say this for your own benefit,** not to lay any restraint upon you, but to promote good order and to secure your undivided devotion to the Lord."
> (1 Corinthians 7:32-35, emphasis added)

In Paul's mind, singleness was freeing—although not in the selfish way that our culture sometimes thinks of it, like marriage is a prison, whereas when you're on your own, you can do whatever you feel like. Rather, it's freeing because you can have a different level of single-minded devotion to God. Married people need to think about how to please and honor their spouses. Marriage often brings children, and so you then have more people that require your devotion, care, and attention. None of that is bad—it's in God's good plan. But it is different than the kind of freedom of focus that comes with singleness.

When you're single, you can enjoy more flexibility in responding to the needs of your friends or pursuing the projects God calls you to. You might be a better listening ear for a friend going through a painful break-up. You might be able to respond more quickly to a crisis that comes up in your family or have more time to spend serving the poor and marginalized. A single person may be able to devote more energy to church work or mission. Of course, married people can also do all those things. But it's more complicated. There are more people impacted by how you spend your time or where you go when you're married or a parent.

Paul says singleness is good—good for you, good for the gospel, and good for the world around you. But that's if you use the gift of singleness not as an excuse to live however you want but as an opportunity to devote your life to single-mindedly following God and doing his will in the world.

SINGLENESS IS NOT LONELINESS

Often people are afraid of staying single because the perception is that being single means being alone. And no one wants to be lonely and left out. But in the kingdom of God, no one is called to be alone. Not only does Jesus offer his constant presence inside us through his Spirit (Romans 8:11); he also gives us the gift of community in his body, the church. The New Testament describes Christians as brothers and sisters (Philippians 4:1). It instructs us to love, care for, encourage, and welcome each other like family (Romans 12:10, 15:7; 1 Corinthians 12:25; 1 Thessalonians 5:11). This is something we do imperfectly, and sometimes better than other times. But in God's design, no one is left lonely, because he has given us each other (see Ephesians 4:1-16).

I had coffee this week with Andrea, a single friend of mine who loves Jesus and the church. While she had stories about times she's felt left out as a single person, she also said, "The church is my family." She told stories about couples who have invited her into their family life; about older women who have been spiritual "mothers" to her; about close friendships with guys—and about her roommate, who cooks dinner for her, travels with her, and knows her well enough to speak to her character and bring up concerns when she sees them. Being single, she said, has given her unique opportunities to drop everything to care for women in need or to speak up for the overlooked. After 15 years of working for a church, she can point to women she's invested in who are now leading others to Jesus. This is the kind of legacy she wants her life to leave, and she prays it will far outlive her.

Ultimately, though, Andrea talked about Jesus. About how he loves her without any of the pitfalls she so frequently hears about in marriage: he always listens, always understands, always has time for her, never leaves. She shared about the times singleness has involved sacrifice but how Jesus has always met her with joy.

MARRIAGE IS HARD!

Singleness is good, according to Scripture. And one of the reasons Paul encourages it is because marriage is hard. He warns, "Those who marry will face many troubles in this life, and I want to spare you this" (1 Corinthians 7:28, NIV).

Yes, marriage is good, and a picture of Jesus, but it is not to be entered into lightly. It's designed by God to be a lifelong commitment, for better or worse, and a sacrificial giving of one's whole self for another. It requires work, sacrifice, devotion, forgiveness, endurance, and humility. I can testify that it's been one of the greatest sources of joy in my life—and one of God's most consistent means of refining me. But if you enter into marriage just for your personal satisfaction or as a "safe" arena for sex, thinking it will be easy, you will be setting yourself up for discouragement. Marriage is full of wonder and full of trouble; it's good, and it's hard; it's receiving, and it's pouring yourself out for someone else.

When you're in a difficult season of life, it can be easy to think that changing your situation will make life better. Singleness can be hard, and it can make marriage look like a better choice. (But being in a hard marriage can make singleness look like an easier choice.) Scripture reminds us that all seasons and stations in life are both hard and good, and that we can both honor Christ and find satisfying joy in him wherever we are. So when it stinks that you're the only one without a date, or when you wonder if you'll be single forever; when you're heartbroken that your significant other broke up with you or bemoaning that your crush doesn't notice you—take it to Jesus. He understands the longings of your heart, and he knows that life is often difficult. He wants to remind us that the answer to life's hard times is not always to change our circumstances but to remember that he is sufficient for them all.

CHRIST IS ULTIMATE
Ultimately, whether God gifts you with singleness or marriage, that status is not your primary identity or your

primary gift. Whatever your position in life, the greatest gift is Jesus, and your greatest identity is being *his*. Our call is to pursue Christ as our highest desire, whether in singleness or marriage.

Sam Allberry, a single pastor, writes:

> "Both marriage and singleness testify to the gospel. Marriage shows us the shape of the gospel in that it models the covenant promises that God has made to us in Christ. Singleness shows us the sufficiency of the gospel because it shows us the reality of what marriage points to—which is our own relationship with Jesus. That is the real marriage. That is the ultimate goal for all of us. Singleness is a way of saying that **because I've got the reality, I don't need the signpost, I don't need the model of it.**" [20]

In other words, single people who model contentment and joy in Christ show us that Jesus is sufficient for our desires—that Jesus is better than anything the world can offer. Including marriage. Including sex.

Singleness, just like marriage, is a gift from God—not to be used selfishly, but for our good and for the good of the world, as we point to the ultimate goodness found in Christ.

FOR REFLECTION

- WHAT WOULD YOU HAVE SAID ABOUT SINGLENESS BEFORE READING THIS CHAPTER?

- HOW HAVE YOUR ASSUMPTIONS BEEN CHALLENGED IN WHAT YOU'VE READ?

"SINGLENESS ... IS A GIFT FROM GOD—NOT TO BE USED SELFISHLY, BUT FOR OUR GOOD AND FOR THE GOOD OF THE WORLD, AS WE POINT TO THE ULTIMATE GOODNESS FOUND IN CHRIST."

- HOW DO YOU THINK GOD IS CALLING YOU, PERSONALLY, TO USE THIS UNMARRIED SEASON OF YOUR LIFE, HOWEVER LONG?

- HOW CAN YOU HONOR HIM IN YOUR CURRENT SITUATION?

Intimacy

WHY IS SEX "GOOD" IN MARRIAGE BUT "BAD" BEFORE IT? ISN'T LOVE LOVE?

"USE YOUR BODY HOWEVER YOU like. No one can tell you what's right for you. Don't listen to the religious people; they're just sex-negative. We support sexual freedom!"

You'll likely have heard at least one of those claims before. Our culture is pushing these ideas all the time. Yet sexuality without limits doesn't actually seem to follow through on these promises. Reports are showing that young adults are actually having less sex than ever (maybe partly because they're putting off marriage), are turning to porn (which leads to problems in real sexual relationships), and are less happy and more depressed.[21] Is it possible this path of sexual freedom is not taking us where we'd hoped to go?

Of course, our culture does acknowledge some sexual limits—that sex isn't *always* acceptable. It's generally agreed that it comes down to consent. It's not ok to rape a stranger, coerce a date, or abuse a child. And it's not ok to get naked in public. But as long as it's between consenting peers in private, the basic message is: you've got freedom to do what you like.

This mindset isn't new. In fact, it's the exact mindset Paul is responding to when he writes this:

> *"'I have the right to do anything,' you say—but not everything is beneficial. 'I have the right to do anything'—but I will not be mastered by anything. You say, 'Food for the stomach and the stomach for food, and God will destroy them both.' The body, however, is not meant for sexual immorality but for the Lord, and the Lord for the body."*
>
> *(1 Corinthians 6:12-13, NIV)*

In other words, while we *are* free to make choices, we're not free from their consequences. In fact, what we feel we "have the right" to do can not only be bad for us ("not everything is beneficial") but can even end up taking over our lives (so that we are "mastered" by it). When it comes to our sexuality, Paul wants us to know that the choices we make with our bodies have significant consequences, both physically and spiritually. He goes on to explain why in the next few verses:

> *"By his power God raised the Lord from the dead, and he will raise us also. Do you not know that your bodies are members of Christ himself? Shall I then take the members of Christ and unite them with a prostitute? Never! Do you not know that he who unites himself with a prostitute is one with her in body? For it is said, 'The two will become one flesh.' But whoever is united with the Lord is one with him in spirit." (v 14-17, NIV)*

The point here is that sex is powerful. It is a strong bond that unites people both physically and spiritually. Since that's so, it is unthinkable for those who are united to Christ to unite our bodies to another person in an unholy way. To misuse sex is destructive—affecting us deeply and undermining our relationship with God. Paul sums it up like this:

> "Flee from sexual immorality. All other sins a person commits are outside the body, but whoever sins sexually, sins against their own body. Do you not know that your bodies are temples of the Holy Spirit, who is in you, whom you have received from God? You are not your own; you were bought at a price. Therefore honor God with your bodies."
>
> (v 18-20, NIV)

There's some strong language in that passage, isn't there? And you might have questions about what exactly Paul means in places. For now, let's just observe that the Bible clearly sets sexuality within limits—and makes it a big deal. Anything powerful needs limits, right? (Think lions, guns, nuclear power plants.) God is watching out for our good.

GLUED TOGETHER

You may have noticed that Scripture uses a lot of "bonding" language around sexuality. The passage we've just read talks about sex uniting people (v 15), the two becoming one in body (v 16), and becoming one flesh (v 16). Usually when this kind of "one flesh" language is used in the Bible (referring back to Genesis 2:24), it's talking about marriage. And marriage is meant to be a lifelong joining of two into one. Sex between a husband and wife is meant to be a bit like glue. It's a physical expression of an enduring commitment to each other, a reuniting that is meant to make the bond stronger.

But Paul, startlingly, uses that same "one flesh" language when he talks about sex with a prostitute. He's warning us that it's not just marriage that creates that kind of bonded union. Sex in any context does that, because it's designed to connect two people emotionally, physically, and spiritually—for good. Sex creates one from two.

This is why sex wasn't designed to be used outside marriage. (This is primarily what Paul means by "sexual immorality.") When two singles have sex, they become like paper that's been glued together; it's not straightforward to neatly separate and be just as they once were. Nothing except marriage provides the guarantee of commitment that sex was designed for. Outside marriage, sex ultimately results in pain and brokenness. Proverbs likens our sexuality to a spring of water—great for drinking from with your spouse but not meant to overflow in the streets (Proverbs 5:15-23). This isn't just a biblical perspective: even *Psychology Today* reports that "the happiness maximizing number of sexual partners is one."[22] The American Psychological Association acknowledges that "Despite their increasing social acceptability ... developing research suggests that sexual hookups may leave more strings attached than many participants might first assume."[23]

The sense of loneliness and shame that can come from giving yourself in such an intimate, vulnerable way to another who later rejects you can leave you feeling depressed and more alone than ever. It can lead to a feeling that your body and your sexuality are of little worth. It can create intimacy challenges later on in marriage. And it can sometimes leave you with lasting physical consequences, too, like STDs or a pregnancy you weren't ready for.

There's a myriad of practical reasons, like a statistically increased chance of a lasting[24] and happy[25] marriage, to practice chastity until marriage. If you've experienced a boyfriend leaving you after you shared your body with him or a girlfriend cheating on you, or if you've had to grapple with STDs or an unwanted pregnancy—and especially if you've been the unwilling victim of sexual assault or abuse—then you know some of the pain that sex misused can cause. (And I'm so, so sorry you've experienced that pain.)

We're urged to *flee* sexual sin (1 Corinthians 6:18). That's not a controlling demand but a fatherly warning. (And in case you're wondering if we're only referring to intercourse, check out the chapters on Screens and Dating for further discussions of the sexual holiness God calls us to.) God, in his wisdom and love, wants us to do whatever it takes to spare ourselves the pain and to save the bond for marriage.

WHAT'S NOT GUARANTEED

But a few important things must be said here. First, while wise choices are more likely to lead to happy outcomes than unwise choices (no surprise here), *choices do not guarantee outcomes*. God nowhere promises a happy, healthy sex life if you save sex for marriage—nor does he even promise marriage. I once met a young woman whose husband died of cancer just a few months into their marriage. I have friends who have desired to be married for decades but find themselves still single. My dear friend Laurie found herself a single mom of an infant when her husband cheated on her repeatedly, leaving her to mourn the loss of her marriage, navigate caring for a baby alone, and wonder what STDs she had been exposed to through no fault of her own.

If we follow the Bible's commands because we want something from it (even a good something, like a healthy marriage), we treat God as a means to an end. We set ourselves up for disappointment when life takes a turn we didn't want. And at some point, it will.

The flipside of the truth that choices do not guarantee outcomes is good news: our unwise or ungodly choices do not doom us to a bad life. God delights to renew and recreate, to heal and repair. Maybe you've already made sexual choices you regret. It can be easy to feel like damaged goods or fear that the ideal that God wanted for you is now beyond your reach. But that's just not true. Yes, there may be lingering consequences from your choices. But God forgives fully anything that we bring to him in repentance. Jesus is the one who makes us pure; none of us can achieve that on our own based on good choices. And God loves to write beautiful new chapters in the stories of our lives—chapters we would never have dreamed of. You are not limited by your past mistakes. God wants to make you a new creation (2 Corinthians 5:17) and lead you to good places (Psalm 23:2-3).

WHAT IS GUARANTEED

God's desire is that we would follow him out of love for him, trust his plans to be good, and find joy in him that nothing in life is able to steal away. That was clearly Paul's perspective when he penned 1 Corinthians 6. He delighted in Jesus and was willing to forgo other pleasures to protect that relationship. Part of our longing for sex is that we desire intimacy: we want to be seen, known, understood, and loved unconditionally. We want to be treasured by someone. Well, God sees and knows us more perfectly than we know ourselves (Psalm 139), and he loves us more deeply than we can begin to understand (Ephesians 3:14-19; Philippians 2:1). A believer's union with Jesus is the strongest and deepest connection we could ever have. Paul says our "bodies are members of Christ himself" and "whoever is united with the Lord is one with him in spirit" (1 Corinthians 6:15, 17, NIV). Our relationship with Jesus is the most intimate and important bond possible. It's worth fighting (or fleeing temptation) to protect.

Being joined to Jesus gives us a new identity: we are his bride, his body, his new creation, a temple of his Spirit. The call, then, is to live out the reality of our new identity, to act as who he's made us to be (Ephesians 2:4-10). Christ's love will always be holy, faithful, generous, sacrificial, unending. That's what he wants us to display in our love, too. When our "love" for another person is really a selfish lust, using someone for our own pleasure— or when it's temporary, fleeting, and unfaithful, not committed for a lifetime—it does not reflect Christ. It dishonors him. And when we choose such things over Christ, it reveals that our primary loyalty is to ourselves and our own happiness rather than to him. It puts something else on the throne, whether that's personal pleasure or another relationship. And that's what the Bible calls spiritual adultery (Ezekiel 23:37; James 4:4-5). It's promising ourselves to Jesus but then living in

> "OUR RELATIONSHIP WITH JESUS IS THE MOST INTIMATE BOND POSSIBLE."

such a way that we give our hearts and bodies to other things. The more we do that, the more we are pulled away from Christ, and the testimony we give to the world is misleading.

However, choosing Jesus over these other desires is a very real way to worship him—to show that he is the one we love most. By pursuing intimacy with him, and by giving up the unholy things that would get in the way, we show the world that Jesus is most valuable.

God may not promise us an easy life, a happy marriage, great sex, or a perfect body in this world. But he does promise us that if we make sacrifices to follow him, we gain Jesus. He will be the most caring companion, faithful husband, and satisfying delight we could ever have. And that is a guarantee we can depend on.

FOR REFLECTION

"SEX IS POWERFUL. IT IS A STRONG BOND THAT UNITES PEOPLE BOTH PHYSICALLY AND SPIRITUALLY ... TO MISUSE SEX IS DESTRUCTIVE—AFFECTING US DEEPLY AND UNDERMINING OUR RELATIONSHIP WITH GOD."

- IF YOU'RE SEXUALLY ACTIVE NOW, WHY? WHAT ARE YOU GAINING, AND WHAT ARE YOU RISKING?

- IF YOU'RE PRACTICING CHASTITY, WHY? DO YOUR REASONS LINE UP WITH GOD'S PROMISES, OR ARE YOU POTENTIALLY SETTING YOURSELF UP FOR DISCOURAGEMENT?

BEING IN RELATIONSHIP WITH JESUS DOESN'T MEAN WE FEEL DEEP SPIRITUAL JOY ALL OF THE TIME—BUT IT DOES MEAN WE HAVE "THE MOST CARING COMPANION, FAITHFUL HUSBAND, AND SATISFYING DELIGHT WE COULD EVER HAVE. AND THAT IS A GUARANTEE WE CAN DEPEND ON."

- IF YOU ARE A CHRISTIAN, HOW HAVE JESUS' FAITHFULNESS AND LOVE IMPACTED YOU SO FAR?

- HOW CAN YOU CONTINUE TO PURSUE A DEEPER RELATIONSHIP WITH HIM?

- IF YOU ARE NOT YET A BELIEVER, HOW DO YOU THINK HAVING SOMEONE LIKE JESUS IN YOUR LIFE—WHO KNOWS YOU BETTER THAN ANYONE AND WILL NEVER RUN OUT ON YOU—WOULD CHANGE YOU?

Orientation

IS THE BIBLE REALLY AGAINST GAY MARRIAGE?

IN THE FIRST THREE CHAPTERS of this book, we saw that God designed our sexuality and our bodies to paint a picture of something much deeper. The lifelong bond and deep intimacy we can experience in marriage are hints at the depth of Jesus' love for us. But it also goes the other way: what we do with our sexuality is supposed to reflect certain truths about that love. This is the background (as we're going to see) to the Bible's repeated affirmations that God has designed marriage as a lifelong, exclusive commitment between a man and a woman.

Now, I realize that this may be hard for you to hear. Our sexual attractions can feel really central to who we are, and any challenge to that feels deeply wounding. If you've experienced same-sex attraction or you're in a gay relationship, you're probably feeling fearful of what I might say, or angry about what you've heard other Christians say already. You may have had very real experiences of people who judged you, shamed you, or simply misunderstood you. Those things hurt, and I'm sorry.

On the other hand, the idea that God prohibits gay marriage might be surprising to you. God is love, so how could he condemn homosexuality? You might think that what I just said about marriage being between a man and a woman simply doesn't make sense.

God *is* love (1 John 4:8). He is the perfection of goodness. He wants what is best for us, and he knows us better than we know ourselves. And he walks beside us as we ask questions and read Scripture and figure out what it all means for our lives. His word, like his nature, is unchanging, trustworthy, and good. So, let's dive in to the Bible and see what God really says about homosexuality.

TELLING A STORY

If you ask Google (or random people on the street) what marriage is or what it's for, you'll get varying answers. Most people will talk about relationship or partnership, love, family, and working together. And all those things are part of it. But according to the Bible, there's a lot more to the story.

From God's perspective, marriage isn't just a formal arrangement or the foundation of a family or even a safe place for sexual expression. It's not simply a means to my personal fulfillment and happiness. Marriage is a story. It's a piece of art. It's a lived experience that's meant to point to something outside ourselves, something far better. It's painting a picture of humanity's relationship with God. When it's wrongly used, then, it distorts this picture. It gives us wrong ideas about God, ourselves, and the story he's writing.

That's why the Bible takes sex and marriage so seriously, rather than leaving it up to us to define as we prefer.

For example: marriage is meant to be a covenant for life because God's love is faithful and unending toward us (Matthew 19:3-6; Malachi 2:14-16; 1 Corinthians 7:10-11, 39). Sex is exclusive between a husband and wife because God's loyal love desires our hearts' worship of him alone (Hosea 2; 1 Chronicles 5:25; Jeremiah 3:20; Song of Solomon 8:6). It is meant to be intimate, joyful, and self-giving because that's the kind of love Christ invites us into (Hosea 2:19-20; Ephesians 5:25-33; John 17:20-26; Colossians 3:19). The sexual relationship between a husband and wife has the power to create new life because it reflects how God's love is creative and life-giving (Genesis 1:28; Malachi 2:15; Romans 4:17). And marriage embraces the "other"—someone fundamentally different than ourselves—because it tells the story of God embracing us (Genesis 2:23-24; Ephesians 5:32; Romans 5:8).

In this grand drama of marriage, a man and a woman are meant to work together, each with a slightly different part to play. (We glimpsed this already in the Gender chapter.) A husband is called to love his wife as Christ loves the church—nourishing, caring, honoring, and giving himself up for her (Ephesians 5:25-33; Colossians 3:19; 1 Peter 3:7). Wives are called to lovingly submit to their husbands out of honor for Christ (Ephesians 5:22-24; Colossians 3:18; 1 Peter 3:1-6; Titus 2:3-5). Some people resist the idea of wives submitting to their husbands, but notice that husbands are called to lay down their lives for their wives! And Jesus himself submitted and served, flipping our idea of what it means to be important (Luke 22:24-27; Philippians 2:5-8; 1 Corinthians 11:3). Submitting does not mean being a doormat, and being the head does not mean getting your way. *Both* spouses have lofty and difficult callings that center on self-giving love and honor for the other. Both callings are a profound invitation to experience the extravagant, sacrificial love of Jesus in a tangible way. And both are essential for marriage to tell an accurate story of Christ and his church.

Gender, then, is indispensable—and not interchangeable—in the marriage covenant. It's an important part of the story God is writing in our relationships. And, since in God's plan sex is reserved for marriage alone, and marriage for a husband and wife, Scripture does not allow for gay relationships (Leviticus 18:22; 20:13; Romans 1:26-27; 1 Corinthians 6:9; 1 Timothy 1:10. You can also turn to the end of the chapter for an extra section on this if you're not yet convinced).

THE SOURCE OF OUR DESIRES

If you identify as gay (or even if you don't), this may sound horribly unfair. Why do people have same-sex desires if that's not what God wants? And how can God get angry at people for desires that they didn't ask for in the first place?

The Bible addresses these topics at most length in Romans 1:18-32. Here, Paul starts by saying that "what can be known about God is plain" (v 18). We're born into a world full of God's glory, where every leaf and snowflake and galaxy point to him as the divine Creator—and so does our sexuality. But, Paul explains, all of us choose in some way to suppress this knowledge and to worship something other than God (v 21-23). He's not talking about choosing gay desires here—he's talking about the instinctive rebellion against God that we all share. In ancient times, people made statues of false gods and bowed down to them. Today we might ignore God as we put all our energy into video games, or dating relationships, or a sport we excel in, or simply our own happiness. In doing so, we've made a terrible trade. We've exchanged what is most powerful, trustworthy, and satisfying (God himself) for the unreliable and temporary stuff of earth.

And God lets us make that choice. In fact, our passage says that when we turn away from him, God gives us up to the lusts of our hearts for impure things (v 24-25). Worshiping created things instead of God means exchanging the truth of God for a lie. And God lets us follow that lie down its path. Our desires get stronger. Our addictions bite harder. Our actions get worse. Our lusts get more overwhelming. God allows us to reap the consequences of our own rebellion against him.

(Of course, God also sent a way out. Jesus came to rescue us from sin—not only from the punishment sin deserves but also from the power it has over us. When we trust in him, we turn away from our rebellion, and we begin a new pattern of life, aided by the Spirit at every turn. But for now, Paul is talking about human nature apart from Jesus. He's sketching a picture of what we are like without Christ.)

It's at this point that Paul talks about homosexuality.

> *"For this reason God gave them up to dishonorable passions. For their women exchanged natural relations for those that are contrary to nature; and the men likewise gave up natural relations with women and were consumed with passion for one another, men committing shameless acts with men and receiving in themselves the due penalty for their error." (Romans 1:26-27)*

Hang with me if you're outraged by the words *dishonorable* or *contrary to nature*. Paul isn't denying that some people experience gay desires that they didn't choose. In using the phrase *contrary to nature*, he's talking about "physical design, not psychological inclination"[26]—in other words, he's referring back to God's created order. In saying *dishonorable*, he's saying that gay sex ignores and therefore dishonors that design.

Paul's point is that gay desires, strong and natural-feeling though they can be, arise from the fall. We didn't choose these desires, any more than we chose the desire to gossip or boast or disobey our parents (just a few of Paul's other examples in verses 28-32). But they are not from God. They are the result of every human's rebellion against God.

And God does hold us accountable for what we do with those desires. We need to recognize that desires for things God has prohibited pull us away from God, not toward him (see chapter 6 for more on this). It's about who we worship—our Creator, or the things he has created. Friends, this is why it's worth it to say no to same-sex desires, wrenching and wounding though that might seem right now. In saying no to those desires, you're saying yes to God.

ORIENTED TOWARD JESUS

Thankfully, we have help in this! When we come to Jesus, whatever we were, we are born again (John 3:3). We are new creations (2 Corinthians 5:17). Following Jesus means "to put off your old self, which belongs to your former manner of life and is corrupt through deceitful desires, and to be renewed in the spirit of your minds, and to put on the new self, created after the likeness of God in true righteousness and holiness" (Ephesians 4:22-24). And that's true of all of us, gay or straight. When we choose to follow Jesus, he gives us strength to turn from our sin—and joy in doing so! His Spirit in us gives us the power both to desire and do his will (Philippians 2:13).

Some people find that their basic attractions do change over time. They experience gay or bisexual desires when they're younger but find that these desires don't define them as adults. Some wind up happily married to a spouse of the opposite sex. (It's more common than you'd think!) Of course, not everyone has that story. Others have tried hard to change their "orientation" and find those temptations stubborn. However, they continue to testify that the power of God is stronger than the pull of temptation and that Jesus is worth all they have given up. Last summer I had the chance to meet Dr. Christopher Yuan, who encountered Jesus while in prison and left his gay lifestyle behind to follow Christ.[27] He'd come to speak at an event I was organizing. Even though it fell on a difficult week (his dad had just died suddenly), through his tears his joy in Christ was so obvious. He was thrilled to be talking with teenagers about Jesus because he knows from experience that Jesus satisfies much more than anything the world offers, including sex, drugs, and money. He doesn't consider following Jesus to be a sacrifice but a pleasure.

> "ULTIMATELY WE ARE EITHER ORIENTED TOWARD GOD OR AWAY FROM HIM."

I don't know what your particular story will be. But one thing is true of all of us. Our "sexual orientation" is not actually a fundamental truth about our identity. Yes, you (like all of us) experience certain desires, but that does not change who you are in God's sight or how he calls you to live. As we mentioned in chapter 6, we tend to talk about orientation in terms of who we're sexually attracted to. But orientation is about what direction we're facing, and ultimately all of us are either oriented toward God or away from him. The closer we draw to Jesus, the more we find that our desires for the things that pull us away from God begin to lessen. They may not disappear, and they may remain a battle. But these battlegrounds are opportunities for us to worship Christ.

Ed Shaw, a pastor who experiences same-sex attraction, wrote:

> "Knowing that God's insistence on sexual union in difference [i.e. marriage is for a man and a woman] is not some silly rule that excludes me but, rather, is part and parcel of the gospel story which includes me and is for my lasting benefit, helps me to live with my sexuality in a way that I can't begin to tell you." [28]

If you experience same-sex desires, you might not be where Ed Shaw is yet. You might disagree with what I've said, or even be upset with me. I get that. If that's you, I urge you to dig into the Scriptures for yourself. And ask God to show you his will. I promise you that if you really discover his heart, you will find it to be good—though perhaps not what you expected.

GIVE GRACE, NOT JUDGMENT

One more thought. It's important to notice that, right after the passage where Paul talks about homosexuality in Romans 1, he immediately tells us that we have no right to judge others (Romans 2:1-3). All of us fall guilty to sin, to treasuring something above Jesus, and so all of us are equally guilty before God and equally deserving of his wrath. And all of us are equally offered grace. Judging others as worse than ourselves shows contempt for God's mercy (v 3-4)—and misses the point of the gospel.

We can be correct to call gay sex a sin and yet deeply hypocritical if we do so without also admitting our own need for a Savior (Luke 6:42)—or if we are not showing those who struggle with same-sex attraction or gender dysphoria the same kind of grace we've been shown. Jesus' grace is undeserved, joyful, inviting, and extravagant, and it woos us to repentance through kindness (Romans 2:4), not condemnation.

My prayer is that the church will be strong enough to hold out the truth, but at the same time known for our love of those who disagree and those who fail. In other words, that we'll be like Jesus. So far we have a long way to go, but I have hope that, by God's grace, you might be the generation to shift that reputation and show the beauty of God's truth and God's good design while at the same time offering love, hope, and grace to those who sin—which includes us all.

EXTRA:
IF YOU'RE NOT CONVINCED...

Not surprisingly, many people disagree with what I've written in this chapter. Some people will tell you that although Old Testament law prohibited homosexuality (see Leviticus 18:22; 20:13), those laws don't count anymore. (After all, we don't keep the Old Testament laws about sacrifices and food from Leviticus 4 and 18). But in reality, the law against homosexuality (as with other laws that concern morality) is valid for us, too. We know this partly because it is based on deep principles that run throughout the Bible, as I've just outlined, but also because it's repeated in the New Testament, showing that it continues to apply to God's people today.

Others will argue that the Bible doesn't condemn homosexuality but simply perversions of it. For example, they say that since there was no concept of sexual orientation in those times, the Bible isn't referring to consensual, committed same-sex relationships. They point out that gay sex in Bible times usually involved men taking advantage of young boys or slaves, or gang rape (such as in the Sodom story in Genesis 19). Certainly, many of the situations the biblical writers recorded included other forms of sexual perversions, like abuse, rape, and pedophilia (see, for example, Judges 19).

But there isn't good biblical reason to assume that, just because homosexuality in Bible times often included other forms of sinful behavior, today's understanding of LGBTQ+ lifestyles would be approved by God. On the contrary, careful biblical interpretation shows that God's call for Christians is still to celibacy in singleness and faithfulness between a husband and wife. Much of this interpretation stems from an understanding of the "why" of God's creation of sexuality, which we've already covered. And some of it is in the text itself. For example, when Leviticus 20:13 condemns men who have sex with men, it says "both of them" have sinned, implying that it was mutual and consensual, not abusive or forced. Romans 1:26-27 talks about men and women who were mutually consumed with desire for "each other" (NLT).

Others point out that the term "homosexual" wasn't in the Bible until 1946, claiming that it was wrongly inserted into the translation by those who had a homophobic agenda. While it's true that Bible translators prior to this time used different language (the word "homosexual" wasn't coined until 1868), the same meaning was there. For instance, the Greek word translated "homosexuality" in 1 Corinthians 6:9 is *arsenokoites*, which comes from the words *arsen* (male) and *koites* (bed)—the same two words found in the Greek translation of the Leviticus law against homosexuality. And Romans 1, though it doesn't use the word "homosexual," clearly describes homosexuality.

Perhaps one of the most moving counterarguments I've heard is when Matthew Vines points to Jesus' teaching that "by their fruit you will recognize them" and claims that the anti-gay teachings in the church have created so much "bad fruit" (that is, negative consequences), they cannot possibly be of God.[29] It's a sobering argument because it's clear the church has caused a lot of harm. Sometimes Christians have alienated people whose sins were different (but no worse) than our own, while we've been blind to our own pride (or hidden sins of pornography and abuse). We have failed to honor people made in God's image, to listen well or love well. And all of those actions have brought a lot of bad fruit. But that does not prove God's word untrue; it proves us all to be sinners in need of grace. It is pride, hate, anger, and fear that have produced a harvest of bad fruit, not truth. The church desperately needs to reclaim the truth of God's word while accurately reflecting Jesus' heart of humility and love for all.

FOR REFLECTION

"MARRIAGE IS A STORY. IT'S A PIECE OF ART. IT'S A LIVED EXPERIENCE THAT'S MEANT TO POINT TO SOMETHING OUTSIDE OURSELVES, SOMETHING FAR BETTER. IT'S PAINTING A PICTURE OF HUMANITY'S RELATIONSHIP WITH GOD. WHEN IT'S WRONGLY USED, THEN, IT DISTORTS THIS PICTURE. IT GIVES US WRONG IDEAS ABOUT GOD, OURSELVES, AND THE STORY HE'S WRITING."

- CAN YOU DESCRIBE HOW THE GENDER DISTINCTION IN MARRIAGE PAINTS A PICTURE OF GOD, AND HOW WRONGLY USED SEXUALITY GIVES US WRONG IDEAS ABOUT GOD?

"WE CAN BE CORRECT TO CALL GAY SEX A SIN AND YET DEEPLY HYPOCRITICAL IF WE DO SO WITHOUT ADMITTING OUR OWN NEED FOR A SAVIOR (LUKE 6:42)—OR IF WE ARE NOT SHOWING THOSE WHO STRUGGLE WITH SAME-SEX ATTRACTION OR GENDER DYSPHORIA THE SAME KIND OF GRACE WE'VE BEEN SHOWN. JESUS' GRACE IS UNDESERVED, JOYFUL, INVITING, AND EXTRAVAGANT, AND IT WOOS US TO REPENTANCE THROUGH KINDNESS."

- IF YOU EXPERIENCE SAME-SEX DESIRES, WHAT KIND OF RESPONSE HAVE YOU EXPERIENCED FROM THE CHURCH? FROM JESUS?

- IF YOU DON'T, HOW HAVE YOU VIEWED OR TREATED LGBTQ+ PEOPLE IN YOUR LIFE? HOW DOES THIS CHAPTER CALL YOU TO CHANGE?

Screens

PORN AND VIRTUAL SEX DON'T HURT ANYONE, RIGHT?

FEWER AMERICAN HIGH-SCHOOLERS ARE HAVING sex than they were thirty years ago, a news headline told me recently. Good news for those of us who believe sex is meant for marriage, right? Except that one of the main reasons for this might be what's in your back pocket. Who needs another person (and the risks that go along with it) when you can find sex on your iPhone?

Pornography (and other kinds of online sex) is more accessible and is more used than ever before. It's easy. It's free. It's almost unavoidable. And it's harmless... or is it?

Here's what Jesus had to say:

> *"You have heard that it was said, 'You shall not commit adultery.' But I tell you that anyone who looks at a woman lustfully has already committed adultery with her in his heart. If your right eye causes you to stumble, gouge it out and throw it*

> *away. It is better for you to lose one part of your body than for your whole body to be thrown into hell." (Matthew 5:27-29, NIV)*

Shocking, isn't it? First of all, Jesus says that just looking at a person lustfully is sexual sin in God's sight. It's very serious. And it's not just a sin against God, but against the person who's become the object of your desires. Jesus is saying that *her sexuality is to be honored, not violated—not even in your mind.*[30] And he underscores this by saying that, hey, if your eye is such a problem that you can't help lustful looks, gouge it out and get rid of it! Better that than get so ensnared in sin that you choose that over Jesus and spend eternity in hell.

I know that doesn't yet sound like good news. It sounds like condemnation. Because which of us has never had a lustful thought or desire? But stick with me. Why does Jesus speak so strongly against the sexual thoughts we harbor in our minds? I think there are several reasons that are worth examining.

WE'RE CALLED TO HONOR PEOPLE

Scripture frequently calls us to honor people. All people (1 Peter 2:17). That girl in the bikini who you think is cute—she's God's creation, made in his image, and her body and sexuality need to be respected. That couple performing sordid sex acts on the web? They're real people, made in God's image and deeply loved by him; they're worthy of honor because they are human.

In order to create the porn that viewers want to see, people (especially women) are being trafficked, sold, drugged, abused, and mistreated. Even when the media is made with their consent (which is a complicated issue anyway—what looks like consent often hides something dark underneath[31]), we cannot love and honor people by using them as sexual objects, even just in our mental fantasies. Porn is *always* dishonoring to the people involved and to the God who created them in his image. It is an abuse of our sexuality, which he designed to be used to love, serve, bring life, and reflect him.

GOD CARES ABOUT OUR MINDS

Romans 8:6 says, "The mind governed by the flesh is death, but the mind governed by the Spirit is life and peace" (NIV). The peace and life Jesus offers involves our minds. But porn pulls our minds away from the Spirit.

Our brains are always learning and changing, a process also known as "rewiring." When parts of your brain fire together, it creates a new connection. The more frequently that happens, the stronger and speedier that wiring becomes—and the more automatic and habitual. This is what allows violinists to play all sorts of notes in quick succession without even thinking about what the notes are. It helps you to ride a bike without thinking about how to pedal, or to drive home without thinking about what street to turn on.

When it comes to porn, frequent viewing trains your brain to associate sexual arousal with seeing bodies on a screen (or worse, seeing sexual violence played out on a screen). That's what you're training your brain to crave. This has unwanted side effects. There has been a sharp increase in erectile dysfunction in young men in recent years, which some studies are attributing at least partly to pornography—because what your brain has "learned" about sex from porn doesn't actually translate to real-life sex with a flesh-and-blood person.[32] Teen boys who are exposed to violent porn are also more than twice as likely to exhibit violent behavior toward their dating partner.[33] And there are connections to increased levels of anxiety, depression, and stress among compulsive pornography users.[34] Porn is not harmless to the viewed or to the viewer. It is dehumanizing to both.

Romans 12:2 says, "Do not be conformed to this world, but be transformed by the renewal of your mind." As believers, we don't want our minds to grow numb to the things that break God's heart. Instead, Jesus wants to renew our minds and capture our attention by his Spirit— enabling our thoughts to reflect his character. We have his help in this! With the Spirit, we can train our brains to see people as neighbors to be loved and served, not as objects to be used selfishly. And this will bring us life and peace.

SEX IS SACRED

Porn wants you to think that sex is about your personal pleasure, the (instant) satisfaction of your urges and desires—divorced from any notion of personhood, soul, sacrifice, or even love. It shows that people can be used (and like it), and that sex is of no consequence. It says that what no one else knows about can't hurt them, and that it's not hurting you. It trains our minds to view our sexuality selfishly.

That's all a lie. As we've seen, the Bible shows sex to have a sacred purpose. It is a bodily re-enactment of one's wedding vows, a giving of oneself wholly to another in love. It's a mutual act of joyful, loving service to the person you have given your life to.

Sex is also a sacred metaphor of God's love for his people. As such, because God's love is holy and faithful, self-sacrificing and life-giving, sex as God designed it is also holy (set apart for marriage), faithful (to one person for life), self-sacrificing (in that you're giving of yourself for your spouse's delight), and life-giving (in that the act of sex can create new life). That's why Scripture says, "Marriage should be honored by all, and the marriage bed kept pure" (Hebrews 13:4, NIV). Single or married, we're called to honor God's sacred design for sexuality—and to honor the humanity of all people, whether those we know or those we see on a screen.

Porn disembodies and cheapens sex. It objectifies and abuses a person. Jesus calls us to hate what is evil and to love, honor, and serve one another above ourselves (Romans 12:9-10).

WHAT ABOUT WITHOUT A SCREEN?

Some people wonder if masturbation is ok if it doesn't involve porn. There are varying opinions (and scenarios) but, biblically, all of the above principles still apply. We're called to train our bodies and our brains to treat sex as sacred and people as honorable. We're called to kill inappropriate desires by whatever drastic means are necessary. (While Jesus probably doesn't *actually* want us to gouge out our eyes, it may not be too extreme to throw away our phones!) And (as we'll see in the next chapter) we're called to develop self-control. While I'd be slow to say "never" to something the Bible doesn't expressly prohibit, I think it's clear that masturbation generally does not fit the above criteria for a holy use of our sexuality.

GOD'S POWER IS ON YOUR SIDE

The devil would love to have you read this, realize that porn is horrible, and feel so much shame about using it that you hide it but still feel powerless to stop it. He knows that sin thrives in the dark, and shame drives us into hiding. It's a cycle that can keep you trapped.

But here's the truth: we all sin. All of us, whether we've used porn or not, have selfishly pursued our own desires at the expense of loving others. God is neither surprised nor horrified at anything you've done. He *delights* to forgive, redeem, and transform.

And if you're ready to make some changes—or set up some protections to keep yourself free from this particular sin—the same power that raised Christ from the dead is at your disposal to help you succeed (Ephesians 1:19-20). But you'll need a battle plan.

STRATEGIES FOR SUCCESS

A football team is unlikely to win if they don't have a game plan in place or if they're unfamiliar with the way the opposing team plays. An army won't win a battle if they don't have the proper weapons and knowledge of where and how the enemy fights. In the same way, to successfully fight the battle against lust, we're going to need a good strategy. This is especially important because temptation is everywhere. You can stream porn or solicit "virtual sex" on a whim from a device in your back pocket. But lust doesn't even need something that hardcore—swimsuits on the beach or billboards for lingerie (or beer or cars), provocative TikTok videos, and even normal PG-13 movies and romance novels can provide plenty of fuel for our minds. We need to be prepared. Here are a few suggestions:

1. **RECOGNIZE THE ROOT**. What situations make you most likely to turn to porn (or other prompts for lust)? Is it when you're tired and lonely, or bored and on your phone in your room, or when you've just seen certain images? And what desires (besides pleasure) might

be underneath that tap of a button? Are you seeking a sense of approval or worth? Or is it comfort or escape? Remember that the only one who can fully satisfy your desires or define your identity is Jesus. Looking for fulfillment elsewhere won't satisfy. But if you recognize what is triggering lust for you, you can be ready to redirect your instincts.

2. **RECREATE HABITS.** The science of habits shows that there's usually a cue (something that triggers the habitual response), the action, and then a "reward" that reinforces the habit. Once you recognize what the cues are for you, you can decide on a new response. When you recognize that you're feeling down, you can go for a walk or shoot hoops to get your blood flowing instead of turning to porn. When you're bored and flicking through your phone, you can decide to open a Bible app or phone a friend. (Or maybe keep your phone outside your bedroom—radical, I know!) Fresh air, the voice of a friend, the knowledge that you're blessing someone else, or the truths of God's love can reinforce your new habit.

3. **ENLIST HELP.** There's a reason God calls the church a body and talks about our need for each other (1 Corinthians 12). You're *much* more likely to be able to fight temptation when you know someone has your back—and when you can't hide. Confessing your sin to a friend who will pray for you and point you to Jesus can be healing (James 5:16). And confessing on the spot when you're dealing with temptation can be even more helpful. Apps like Fortify, Canopy, or Covenant Eyes* can be great tools, as well. A friend

---

* Check out covenanteyes.com, accountable2you.com, joinfortify.com, canopy.us, and fightthenewdrug.org.

of mine says she reads the parent ratings on movies before she watches them, to make sure it won't be something that will start her desires down a wrong path. These are all great tools! But there's something more essential.

4. **LOOK TO JESUS.** Tools and strategies can only go so far. Scripture encourages us that if we want to throw off the sin that so easily entangles, we need to fix our eyes on Jesus (Hebrews 12:1-2). It's when we keep the real prize in mind—the reward of intimacy with Christ and pleasures forevermore—that we can find the stamina to keep running when the going gets tough, when the fruit looks good, when our bodies feel weak. Looking to Jesus reminds us that he is truly better, that he gives what we need to stand strong (Ephesians 6:10-18), and that the battle is worth it. When you feel tempted, opening your Bible can remind you of the reasons you are resisting, the help that's on your side, and the prize that awaits (for example, check out Psalm 24; Psalm 101:1-3; 1 Corinthians 10:13; Philippians 3; and Hebrews 11:32 – 12:29).

Your generation is facing a bigger porn problem than ever before, due to how prevalent and easy it is, but I believe you can also be the generation to take a stand. You can fight for the rights of the exploited. You can defend the honor of people made in God's image. You can create communities where it's safe to talk about your struggles and where you pray for and help each other. You can confess your failings and find abundant forgiveness in Christ. You can protect the integrity of your sexuality, and by your life and your words show others that God's pattern is truly better.

FOR REFLECTION

- IF YOU STRUGGLE WITH PORN, ASK YOURSELF THE QUESTIONS IN "RECOGNIZE THE ROOT" AND SEE IF YOU CAN IDENTIFY THE ROOT OF THE ISSUE FOR YOURSELF.

- THEN ASK: WHAT NEW HABITS CAN I FORM TO RE-TRAIN MY BRAIN? WHAT HELP WILL I NEED IN PLACE?

"YOU'RE MUCH MORE LIKELY TO BE ABLE TO FIGHT TEMPTATION WHEN YOU KNOW SOMEONE HAS YOUR BACK—AND WHEN YOU CAN'T HIDE."

- WHO CAN YOU TALK WITH ABOUT YOUR REAL-LIFE STRUGGLES AND VICTORIES (WHETHER OVER PORN OR ANYTHING ELSE)? ARE THEY TRUSTWORTHY AND QUICK TO PRAY WITH YOU AND POINT YOU TO JESUS?

- IF NOT, WHO CAN YOU INVITE INTO THAT LEVEL OF RELATIONSHIP?

Dating

WHAT CAN AND CAN'T WE DO?

I'M SURE THIS IS THE chapter some of you have been waiting for since the beginning. What does all of this *actually mean* for when I'm with my boyfriend or girlfriend? How far is too far? What does God want us to do?

Dating can be a fun and exciting season of life! But it can also be a time with a lot of temptation—and a lot of pain and heartache if done wrong. Even people who are committed to honoring God in their relationships can find it confusing and challenging to navigate dating; I know several godly friends who look back on those years with regret. So what does the Bible have to say to us about relationships?

If you're searching the Bible for a list of dating dos and don'ts, you're not going to find it. Dating as we think of it today wasn't a thing back then. (Most marriages were arranged!) But there *are* plenty of principles that apply to your dating life. For example, here's 1 Thessalonians 4:3-7:

> *"For this is the will of God, your sanctification: that you abstain from sexual immorality; that each one of you know how to control his own body in holiness and honor, not in the passion of lust like the Gentiles who do not know God; that no one transgress and wrong his brother in this matter ... For God has not called us for impurity, but in holiness."*

What God is after is our sanctification, or holiness: being set apart as his people and becoming like him in his character. He calls us away from lust, immorality, and harming others, and toward holiness, self-control, honor, and love. There's a lot in those few short verses! And the rest of Scripture has more to say, too. So here's my attempt at distilling some key principles from the Bible into practical reminders for our dating lives as believers.

SHOW HONOR

Honor is a common theme in the Bible. Of course, we are called to honor God in everything we do (Revelation 4:11). But Christians are also called to honor everyone else (1 Peter 2:17). Romans 12:10 says, "Love one another with brotherly affection. Outdo one another in showing honor." That's quite a high calling: to honor others more than we expect to be honored, to seek their honor more than our own desires. We do this because it reflects what God is like. It creates the kind of community he designed for his church. And it honors him. So what does it practically look like to honor someone, particularly the person you're dating?

It means that the way we talk to and about our significant other shows respect, gentleness, and care. It means honoring their boundaries and making sure you're not putting your date in a position where they're uncomfortable. It means treating their body as something precious, something you will work to protect and not exploit.

Paul urges us to remember that in Jesus we are a family. You're called to honor the wisdom of the godly older people around you—the ones who instruct you in God's word and set you an example. Don't just scorn their remarks as old-fashioned. As for younger people (including those you date), you are to regard them as brothers and sisters in Christ, to be honored and treated with absolute purity (1 Timothy 5:1-2).

If you're in a relationship, it's a good idea to pause regularly and ask: How have I been showing honor to my boyfriend/girlfriend? Are there any ways in which I've dishonored him or her, perhaps unintentionally? Is our relationship honoring God?

CAUSE NO HARM

Secondly, God asks us to cause no harm. Don't skip over this because it feels obvious. I know that you know you shouldn't hurt the person you're dating. But this call goes deeper than a surface-level understanding of harm.

There's an interesting snippet from the book of Proverbs that's worth pondering:

> "Three things are too wonderful for me;
>   four I do not understand:
> the way of an eagle in the sky,
>   the way of a serpent on a rock,
> the way of a ship on the high seas,
>   and the way of a man with a virgin."
>   (Proverbs 30:18-19)

This may seem like nice poetry but not super insightful. What do those four things have in common? There's beauty? An element of mystery? True, but my *ESV Study Bible* notes pointed out that there's more going on. The clue is in the following verse, which is linked with the repeated word "way":

> *"This is the way of an adulteress:*
> *she eats and wipes her mouth*
> *and says, 'I have done no wrong.'"*
> (Proverbs 30:20)

The adulteress says she's done nothing wrong, but it's clear that that's not God's perspective: adultery always leaves a trace, always causes harm. The images in the previous verses, meanwhile, all show movements that happen *without* leaving a trace. An eagle doesn't leave trails in the sky. A snake doesn't leave footprints on a rock. A sailboat doesn't leave marks on the waves. What about "the way of a man with a virgin"—what does that have in common with snakes and sailboats? In this example, too, no trace is left. The adulteress causes harm, but the godly man does not. He leaves no wounds on his date's body or her heart.

My family just spent a week in Arches National Park, which is full of gorgeous red rock scenery and soft sand. There were signs everywhere warning us to watch where our feet stepped. It turns out there's an almost invisible biological soil crust there, made of tiny organisms that grow slowly on the sand. A single footprint can damage it to the point where it takes years to grow back.

That's a good way to think about dating: tread carefully. Leave no trace. Damage caused may be slow to heal.

Hearing this, your mind may jump to the most obvious

examples. Having sex with your girlfriend can leave her pregnant, share STDs, or leave emotional hurt if you break up. All true. But that's a simplistic view of sex. There are a lot of steps in between celibacy and intercourse. (Is kissing ok? What about making out? Messing around with clothes on? Oral sex?) Well, Ephesians 5:3 tells us there must not be "even a hint of sexual immorality" (NIV). In God's design, *all* sexual expression is to be reserved for your spouse. If you're not married to someone, they're not your spouse (duh). Those who are not your spouse are your neighbors, or (if they're believers) your brothers and sisters—they're to be treated with absolute purity.

Of course, while the principle is clear in Scripture, some of the specifics of what constitutes "absolute purity" need to be individually figured out. Different people choose different guidelines for their dating relationships. Some friends decided they would cap their kisses at ten seconds while dating so they didn't risk getting carried away into anything further. One couple followed advice to only show physical affection that they would also be comfortable showing in public—so maybe a long kiss, but nothing that would be awkward or questionable for a stranger walking by. Others have decided that if it's not a kiss, hug, or touch they would give a sibling, it should be saved for a spouse.

These kinds of boundaries may sound like dampers on the fun of dating. But they're for our good! All of the touch that's meant to turn us on and draw us to another person is intended to culminate in sex—and it's a beautiful progression in marriage, where you have full freedom to go there without fear or shame. But outside of marriage, even hints of sex are dangerous. It's easy to slip into more than you planned on. Going too far creates emotional connections that can leave real pain if you break up. Part of honoring your significant other and keeping them from harm is ensuring that you are not a part of leading them into sin, creating emotional hurt, or making promises with your body that neither of you are ready to make with your lives.

It's also worth stating: if the person you're dating tries to push your boundaries or ignores your "no," it's not a healthy, loving relationship. Someone who cares about you should always respect what you're comfortable with. If not, it's time for (at minimum) a clear conversation about boundaries or a pause in the relationship for your protection.

Consider: Is the way you touch, talk, dress, or act honoring and protecting the integrity of your boyfriend or girlfriend? When you are with them, are you nudging each other toward holiness or making it harder? What can you do to ensure that if you broke up tomorrow, they could say that you brought them honor and caused no harm?

PRACTICE SELF-CONTROL AND PATIENCE

There are some character traits that everyone tends to admire, like courage and persistence. Self-control and patience probably don't make that list—maybe because they're only obvious when they're painfully absent. However, they're crucial if we want to resist temptation and honor God with our sexuality. Our ability to patiently wait on God's timing and to control our impulses has implications for all of life and will set us on a path toward a good life or toward ruin (Proverbs 25:28). But self-control and patience do not come naturally; they must be practiced. (And let's be real: the phones in our pockets and the schedules of our lives will train us in the opposite if we're not careful, so that our lives will be marked by hurry and instant gratification.)

We can practice patience and self-control by resisting our sexual impulses. But it's wisest to practice *before* we are put in a difficult position. Fasting (from food or from other things we desire, like screens or shopping) is one practice that trains us in self-control.* Developing God-honoring habits around what we watch and listen to and what we allow our mind to think about will also help us when sexual temptation is strong. When we practice patience, we reflect God, who is patient with us (2 Peter 3:9), and we open the door for God to do a work in us that requires sustained time.

Ask yourself: How am I intentionally practicing self-control and patience? Is there anything unintentional in my life that is training me to be impatient?

LOVE SACRIFICIALLY, LIKE JESUS

We most often think of love as a feeling. We love the people we like, the ones who make us feel happy. And so it's easy to say we love the person we're dating because (usually) we love the way we feel around them. But is that all that love is? When the Bible describes love, it describes service (Galatians 5:13), perseverance (1 Corinthians 13:7), and sacrifice (John 15:13). Real love is always about seeking someone else's interests ahead of our own. Or as Tim Keller puts it, "True love meets the needs of the loved one no matter the cost to oneself. All life-changing love is some kind of substitutionary sacrifice."[35] It's taking on the cost so that the one you love doesn't have to.

Jesus, of course, displayed the ultimate love when he gave his life for us. He calls us to follow in his example,

* There are certain people for whom it's not healthy to fast from a meal, like those with diabetes or an eating disorder. If you're unsure, ask a doctor, or choose something else to fast from.

loving others not because it's convenient and makes us feel good, but as a way of displaying his sacrificial, life-giving love toward others (Ephesians 5:1-2). Love, then, is not about taking or feeling but about giving. And in real life, that often means giving something up for the good of another. In a God-honoring dating relationship, it means considering what's best for the other person and for the kingdom of God rather than what we most want. An important part of that is seeking their sexual integrity and not asking for sexual fulfillment from someone you're not married to. As Jared Kennedy wrote:

> *"If a young man asks a girl to give him her body before he's willing to give her his life in marriage, that's manipulation. Real love is the self-giving love of Christ, not premarital sex ... Only within the covenant union, where our commitments have already been made, are we safe to be vulnerable and experience the free gift of intimacy without thinking love must be earned."* [36]

It's possible these words may bring a sense of guilt or sadness for you. Maybe you've already made decisions you regret; maybe you've been taken advantage of in ways you never wanted. Remember, there is nothing God will not forgive and heal if we ask him! And it's also never too late to start again, or start making different choices.

If you're dating, consider: Do I tend to think about love in terms of feelings or actions? Is there anything God might be asking me to give up in order to love my

"LOVE, THEN, IS NOT ABOUT TAKING OR FEELING BUT ABOUT GIVING."

significant other better? How can I convey the servant-hearted, self-giving love of Christ to him or her?

FIND CONTENTMENT IN JESUS

Ultimately, any time we're tempted to sin, it's because we're discontented. In the moment of desire, we don't feel like Jesus is enough for us. Like Eve, we feel like he's holding out on us, that something else would be better. If we feel like we need to compromise with a person we're dating so that they'll stay with us, or if sexual desire is taking over our thoughts, or if we're miserable because we don't have a date—all of this is evidence that we've lost sight of Jesus and how all-satisfying he is.

The best way to cultivate a healthy dating relationship, then, is to make sure your relationship with Christ is healthy. When you're connected to him, delighting in his abundant love, you can enjoy dating as a chance to get to know someone, have fun together, and find out whether you'd help each other live out God's calling together. You don't need the other person to fulfill you or bring you happiness because you already have all that in Jesus. You're free to love them, selflessly and even sacrificially, patiently and purely, because that's the kind of love you've received. And if you fall short, you can find forgiveness and a clean start in the unshakable love of God.

Ask yourself: Is my dating relationship helping me to love Christ more or competing for my affections? Am I content in God's love, whether or not I have a date? What can I do to invest in strengthening my relationship with Jesus?

BE SET APART

God's will, Paul says, is our sanctification (1 Thessalonians 4:3): he wants us to become holy. That's a rather churchysounding word, but it means to be set apart. To have a higher purpose. To be different from the world around us. To be pure. Ultimately God is the one who is truly holy, and when we become holy, we're becoming like him. We're reflecting his character, his love, and his wisdom in increasing ways.

What does this mean for our dating lives? At a practical level, one of the ways we're called to be "set apart" is by dating only other believers. Because marriage brings such a strong and sacred union between two people, it's essential that they share a common first love—that is, Christ (see 1 Corinthians 7:39; 2 Corinthians 6:14-18). When two people who don't even agree on the purpose of life, what has most value, or how you determine right from wrong, are joined as "one flesh," the relationship is set up for frustration and compromise. Usually, this results in the believer giving up their faith (or at least significant practice of it) to accommodate the unbeliever. The Bible is full of stories of people who shipwrecked their faith by marrying someone who didn't worship the same God, and God warns us strongly not to do this (Deuteronomy 7:3-6; 1 Kings 11:1-10; Malachi 2:11-12). I've known people who thought they could be an exception—who thought they had found someone respectful of their beliefs, and that they could marry them and keep their own faith. I've never seen it work.

When it comes to our sexuality, choosing to live holy lives is going to make us "set apart" because we're not going to think or act like most of the people around us. It's going to show up in our attitudes toward our bodies and toward other people, including those we date. It's going to show up in an unpopular commitment to celibacy while single and in protecting our eyes and minds from media content that compromises our sexual integrity.

It's likely going to earn you some questions—and maybe confused looks. But all of this is an opportunity to share with others the better hope, better joy, and better love you have in Jesus.

FOR REFLECTION

- IF YOU'RE DATING, REVIEW THE QUESTIONS AT THE END OF EACH SECTION AND ASK GOD IF THERE ARE ADJUSTMENTS YOU COULD MAKE IN YOUR RELATIONSHIP TO HONOR HIM (OR YOUR DATE) MORE.

- IF YOU'RE NOT DATING, MAKE A LIST OF GOALS OR GUIDELINES YOU WOULD WANT FOR A FUTURE RELATIONSHIP (AND RED FLAGS OF AN UNHEALTHY RELATIONSHIP).

"LOVE, THEN, IS NOT ABOUT TAKING OR FEELING BUT ABOUT GIVING. AND IN REAL LIFE, THAT OFTEN MEANS GIVING SOMETHING UP FOR THE GOOD OF ANOTHER. IN A GOD-HONORING DATING RELATIONSHIP, IT MEANS CONSIDERING WHAT'S BEST FOR THE OTHER PERSON AND FOR THE KINGDOM OF GOD RATHER THAN WHAT WE MOST WANT."

- WHAT EVIDENCE OF GODLINESS, HONORING, AND SELF-CONTROL WOULD YOU LOOK FOR IN A POTENTIAL DATE?

- HOW CAN YOU GROW IN THESE AREAS PERSONALLY?

Abuse

WHAT ABOUT WHEN I DIDN'T HAVE A CHOICE?

SEX IS MEANT TO BE beautiful, a picture of God's sacrificial love for us—but sadly, sometimes it's the exact opposite. Sometimes it's forced, selfish, and abusive, and it leads to deep pain and trauma. Statistics estimate that somewhere between a quarter and a fifth of teens have been sexually abused, often by someone they knew and trusted.[37] Instead of sex modeling love, deepening intimacy, and creating joy, sexual abuse models an utter lack of care for another and leaves hurt, shame, and brokenness in its place. The depth of the pain that abuse victims feel is itself an indicator of how significant our sexuality is. As Sam Allberry points out:

> *"The pain of sexual assault is not the pain of a grazed knee but the trauma of a holy space being desecrated. Maybe our bodies are less like playthings and more like temples."* [38]

Abuse, then, is a tool of Satan, who seeks to steal, kill, and destroy (John 10:10) and to use for harm what God designed for good. If you have suffered or are currently suffering the trauma of abuse, you know it can have ripple effects in your life for years to come. That's why it's so important to seek out help. Healing from abuse can be a long and painful journey—but it is possible, because God is the Healer (Exodus 15:26; Matthew 4:23).

I am not a therapist, and even if I were, helping people find healing from abuse is beyond the scope of a single book chapter. If you have been or are the victim of abuse, I encourage you to confide in a trusted adult and, if you can, seek out help from someone skilled at bringing both God's word and practical counsel to abuse situations. But what I do hope to accomplish in this chapter is to help you start to see abuse from God's perspective: to know how deeply loved you are, and to see the hope of healing that he offers.*

WHAT IS ABUSE?

Sometimes it's obvious that abuse has taken place. At other times, there may be acts that you were uncomfortable with, but you aren't sure if they were abuse or not. In the US, when you are a minor (under 18), *any* kind of sexual activity or exposure from an adult (including situations that don't involve physical contact) is considered sexual abuse. Sometimes the abuser will convince you that you asked for

---

* Note for youth leaders: This is a good opportunity to review your church's policies to ensure that you have a clear plan for ensuring student safety at church events and responding to abuse situations that are brought to your attention, whether from within or outside the church. For practical help and tools, see churchcares.com and ecap.net, or in the UK, thecss.co.uk.

it or wanted it, but that's a form of manipulation. Minors aren't old enough to give consent, so sexual activity from an adult is *always* abuse.[39] It's also always illegal. (Similar but slightly different laws apply in other countries.) Over-18s, of course, can be sexually abused as well, if they don't give consent to the activity. And abuse or rape can also come from a peer—it can even be the person you're dating, if they don't respect your "no" or wait for consent.

If you've been put in that situation, it's important to seek out help—either from a trusted adult you know, or from an anonymous helpline.* It's also important to know God sees, cares deeply, and is able to heal.

GOD STANDS WITH YOU

Abuse is usually done in secret. No one sees; no one seems to understand your pain. You may not feel like you know who to tell or what they'll think if you do talk about it. While inviting others into your story will be part of the healing journey, the starting point is understanding that God sees your pain. It is not hidden from him. He weeps with you.

We are told that God records the miseries of his people in a book and collects our tears in his bottle (Psalm 56:8). He is near to the brokenhearted and saves those who are crushed in spirit (Psalm 34:18). He does not bring shame, disgust, disappointment, or doubt to our pain but immense love and concern.

Throughout the Bible we see God's heart for the afflicted, particularly those who have been taken advantage of by the powerful. He is the Helper and Defender of the weak, who listens to the cry of the victim and defends

* In the US, rainn.org; in the UK, childline.org.uk; in Australia, 1800respect.org.au.

the oppressed (Psalm 10:14-18). The law continually reminded God's people not to take advantage of the powerless because God himself would be their Defender (Leviticus 19:14;Proverbs 23:10-11). Jesus met the sick, the oppressed, and the rejected with gentleness and love, and it was said, "A bruised reed he will not break, and a smoldering wick he will not quench, until he brings justice to victory" (Matthew 12:20). If you've suffered at the hands of others, God sees you and he stands with you, full of compassion, gentleness, and hope.

GOD CALLS ABUSERS TO ACCOUNT

One of the most awful things about abuse is that the sufferer is often made to feel that it's their fault. Abusers are skilled at controlling the storyline and brainwashing others, including the victim. And sometimes well-meaning people who hear about abuse further confuse things by the types of questions they ask or comments they make. Then, on top of the pain of abuse, victims deal with shame, wondering if they could have prevented it.

Please hear this: if you have been abused, *it is not your fault.* It does not change your worth, value, or dignity. And it does not have to define your story. God is both the Healer of the broken,

"GOD SEES YOU AND HE STANDS WITH YOU, FULL OF COMPASSION, GENTLENESS, AND HOPE."

full of kindness and compassion, and the Judge, who brings justice and calls abusers to account. While he is full of gentleness and compassion toward the wounded, he has harsh words for those who use their power to oppress or harm others (see Psalm 14:4-5; Isaiah 3:14-15 and 10:1-3).

Abuse is perhaps darkest of all when it happens at the hands of those entrusted with our care: when parents abuse the children they're called to protect, or spiritual leaders abuse those under their shepherding. Sadly, these situations are not uncommon. And to make matters worse, they've often been mishandled, even in the church. But God warns that those given authority who harm people under their care will face a harsh judgment (see Ezekiel 34; James 3:1; Luke 12:48). The church must take a stand, with God, on behalf of the hurting and against those who abuse (1 Corinthians 5; Proverbs 24:11-12).

GOD IS THE HEALER

Abuse or assault brings significant trauma that can affect every area of your life. But it does not have to determine your identity or your future. God delights to be the Healer and Restorer. It's who he is!

God's healing almost always comes about in community, which is why the devil loves to keep you isolated. If you've experienced abuse and it's still in the dark, I encourage you to find some trusted people to tell, so that they can pray for you, help you find care, and start the healing process (James 5:16). This is important whether it was recent or long ago—and especially important if it's ongoing. God wants you to reach a place where his love frees you from fear (Psalm 23:4), shame (Isaiah 54:4; 61:7), and bitterness (Hebrews 12:15), and where you can regain a view of sexuality (and of your body) as something beautiful and holy.

God sees you. He loves you immensely and stands by as your Defender. He will bring all abusers to account. And this is what he delights (and promises) to do:

"To bind up the brokenhearted ...
* to comfort all who mourn;*
to grant to those who mourn in Zion—
* to give them a beautiful headdress*
*   instead of ashes,*
the oil of gladness instead of mourning,
* the garment of praise instead of a faint spirit;*
that they may be called oaks of righteousness,
* the planting of the Lord,*
*   that he may be glorified.*
They shall build up the ancient ruins;
* they shall raise up the former devastations;*
they shall repair the ruined cities,
* the devastations of many generations ...*
Instead of your shame there shall be
* a double portion;*
* instead of dishonor they shall rejoice in their lot;*
therefore in their land they shall possess
* a double portion;*
* they shall have everlasting joy." (Isaiah 61:1-7)*

If you've suffered abuse, I pray that this chapter can give you a small dose of hope. I pray you have courage to tell a trusted adult, if you haven't yet (and to keep trying until you find someone who really listens). I pray that you can find a place of safety if you're currently experiencing abuse. That you can find trusted and godly adults to wisely walk you through the trauma you've experienced until you find hope and healing on the other side. That God will redeem your story and, in your healing and comfort, that you find abundant joy and freedom. And that your redeemed story can bring hope to others who suffer, too.

FOR REFLECTION

"WE ARE TOLD THAT GOD RECORDS THE MISERIES OF HIS PEOPLE IN A BOOK AND COLLECTS OUR TEARS IN HIS BOTTLE (PSALM 56:8). HE IS NEAR TO THE BROKENHEARTED AND SAVES THOSE WHO ARE CRUSHED IN SPIRIT (PSALM 34:18)."

- HOW HAVE YOU EXPERIENCED GOD'S NEARNESS OR CARE IN YOUR TIMES OF PAIN?

- IF YOU'RE CURRENTLY IN A DARK TIME, HOW CAN YOU INVITE GOD'S PRESENCE AND ACCEPT HIS CARE?

"IF YOU HAVE BEEN OR ARE THE VICTIM OF ABUSE, I ENCOURAGE YOU TO CONFIDE IN A TRUSTED ADULT AND, IF YOU CAN, SEEK OUT HELP FROM SOMEONE SKILLED AT BRINGING BOTH GOD'S WORD AND PRACTICAL COUNSEL TO ABUSE SITUATIONS."

- IF YOU'VE BEEN THE VICTIM OF ABUSE OR ASSAULT, HAVE YOU TOLD ANYONE? HOW DID THEY RESPOND?

- IF YOU HAVEN'T YET RECEIVED HELP, WHO MIGHT BE ABLE TO START YOU ON THAT HEALING JOURNEY?

Conclusion

IT'S WORTH THE COST

ONCE, WHEN JESUS WAS TRYING to help his disciples understand what it meant to follow him, he told this story:

> *"The kingdom of heaven is like treasure hidden in a field, which a man found and covered up. Then in his joy he goes and sells all that he has and buys that field." (Matthew 13:44)*

In this parable, the man stumbles upon hidden treasure and instantly realizes its value. It is worth more than he can imagine, far more than the combined value of all his assets. So he does what makes sense: he sells all his stuff, buys the field, and becomes the new owner of this buried treasure. And he does all this *in his joy*. He eagerly gives up everything he has because he knows what it will gain him. It might cost him everything, but it makes him a billionaire.

MORE TO THE STORY

That, Jesus says, is the kingdom of God. It's not cheap. It's not easy. But the treasure you get in the end far outweighs anything you give up. And that includes sex.

I don't know how you're feeling as we end this book. Maybe you're excited to walk with Jesus. Or maybe it feels a bit overwhelming. Maybe you feel guilt over some past choices, or you're still not persuaded about some things I've said. Or maybe you are convinced, but it seems hopeless to try to live it out.

Sometimes following Jesus can feel too hard. Isn't Jesus asking us to give up a lot? Is it really worth it? Is it even possible?

The answer to all three of those questions is *yes, absolutely!*

IT'S COSTLY

There's no denying that Jesus asks us to give up a lot. In fact, when Jesus called his disciples, they left *everything* to follow him (Luke 5:11, 28; Mark 10:28; Philippians 3:8). Some of them eventually lost their lives. Jesus even said, "Those of you who do not give up everything you have cannot be my disciples" (Luke 14:33, NIV). Walking with Jesus involves a daily dying to self, taking up your cross, and following him (Luke 9:23).

Central to the call of the gospel is repentance (Mark 1:15), which means to turn away from what we used to chase and turn to God. As J. D. Greear puts it, "It means being willing to walk away from anything and everything in your life that competes with Jesus."[40] For some, that will mean crucifying your desires for pornography or gay sex; for others it will mean crucifying your right to determine your own identity, to have a certain relationship, to make a lot of money, to be popular. But *for all of us, it costs everything.* In following Jesus, we lay down the right to call the shots for our lives. We choose not to be identified by our sexuality, ambitions, or gifts, but to be identified as servants of Jesus Christ. This central identity then shapes everything else about our lives.

IT'S WORTH IT

But it's worth it, a hundred times over. Just like in the parable of the hidden treasure, we might have to give up a lot, but the reward we gain is far greater. As the Bible puts it, "This light momentary affliction is preparing for us an eternal weight of glory beyond all comparison" (2 Corinthians 4:17).

Ultimately, the reward I've been trying to point to throughout this book isn't heterosexuality, or marriage, or a comfortable life, or any of that. If we focus on those benefits, we miss the much bigger story God is writing through our sexuality. We miss the better treasure: a good God who invites you into intimacy and love deeper than anything the world can offer.

The hope for those who experience same-sex attraction isn't heterosexuality but Jesus. The hope for the lonely isn't marriage but Jesus. The reality is that, whatever the struggle, Jesus may choose to heal it, and he may not. He can heal, of course. But often, in the mystery of his wisdom and love, he chooses simply to remind us that his grace is sufficient, even for this (Philippians 3:7-10).

> "THERE IS A BETTER TREASURE: A GOOD GOD WHO INVITES YOU INTO INTIMACY AND LOVE."

Rather than placing our confidence in working for awesome sexual experiences, a great marriage, or material prosperity (which are all temporary), we want to build our lives on the kingdom that can't be shaken. We want the faith of Shadrach, Meshach, and Abednego, who knew that God *could* rescue them from the fire but were committed to following him even if he did not because they saw God himself as a better prize (Daniel 3:17-18). Or the faith of Paul, who said, "Indeed, I count everything as loss because of the surpassing worth of knowing Christ Jesus my Lord. For his sake I have suffered the loss of all things and count them as rubbish, in order that I may gain Christ" (Philippians 3:8). Self-denial, suffering, and patient endurance are part of walking with Jesus in a broken world and with a body that still battles sin. But life is short. Eternity awaits.

In eternity we will experience the ultimate marriage: that of Christ the Bridegroom with his bride, the church. Feasting, beauty, treasure, and joy await that our minds cannot begin to comprehend. But we get a taste of these things now because, as believers, we can have God's Spirit inside us. We can enjoy intimacy with our Savior. We can rest in the confidence that he forgives us whenever we ask. We can cling to a hope stronger than death, a joy untouched by suffering, a peace that surpasses understanding. We have a Guide and a Friend who will walk with us through all of life. We have a new family in the faith, a truth we can build our lives on, and a confident hope that eternity with our Bridegroom will be better than our wildest dreams.

That's what our sexuality is meant to point toward. That's what the Bible is telling us throughout its story. That's what all of life is about.

And it's better by far than anything we leave behind to gain it.

IT'S POSSIBLE

You may be thinking, "That sounds beautiful, but I'm still not sure I can do it." The thought of going through life single and celibate, or with a gender that feels disorienting, or never looking at porn again, or acting in a holy way with the person you're dating, can feel not just overwhelming but impossible. I get that! On one level, it's true: living a life of holiness is completely beyond our reach—on our own.

But we *aren't* left on our own.

What is impossible for us is possible for God (Luke 18:27). Jesus has already defeated sin and death, and as believers we have his Holy Spirit living inside us (1 Corinthians 3:16). We aren't asked to fight sin in our own strength. It's the Spirit's job to transform both our desires and our lives for God's glory (Philippians 2:13). He is the one who guards us, keeps us, guides us, teaches us, and empowers us. And he will never stop pursuing our hearts. That means there's even space to be happy about the things we find hard, because in them we can experience the very power of God (2 Corinthians 12:9-10).

Hebrews 12:1 encourages us:

> *"Let us throw off everything that hinders and the sin that so easily entangles. And let us run with perseverance the race marked out for us, fixing our eyes on Jesus." (NIV)*

It's true that sin easily trips us up. Throughout this book I've been encouraging you to throw those sins off—and maybe that's been hard to hear at times. But when we feel uncertain or weak or frustrated or burdened (and even when we don't feel any of those things!), what's crucial is to fix our eyes on Jesus. He is the only one who can help us throw off the weight of overwhelming sins. He is the greater treasure. He is the better Bridegroom. And he is the one who makes us holy. We just need to keep listening to him, trusting his word, and asking for his help.

So yes, make every effort to live in holiness. It's worth anything you have to give up. Fight sin, to the death, because the joy Jesus offers is infinitely worth it. But do it keeping your eyes on Jesus, remembering that he's the one who scored the victory, and it's his strength that allows us to win the battle.

I don't know where you were with Jesus when you started this book, and I don't know what you're feeling now that you've finished. But I hope you've seen a glimpse of Jesus as the treasure that he is. I hope you've seen that there is more to the Bible's story than you realized, and that it is truly good news. I hope you continue to get to know Jesus, to read his word, to follow him. I believe that as you trust him with your deepest longings, you will find him more than able to satisfy.

> *"Now may the God of peace himself sanctify you completely, and may your whole spirit and soul and body be kept blameless at the coming of our Lord Jesus Christ. He who calls you is faithful; he will surely do it." (1 Thessalonians 5:23-24)*

WITH GRATITUDE

AS I LOOK BACK ON how this book took shape, I'm deeply grateful for the many people who influenced both my life and its words.

First, to my parents, Kim and Roger Ooms. Mom, you were the first to teach me to love and study the Bible, as well as to write, and you've been a constant encouragement. Dad, your unconditional love instilled confidence and modeled Christ. Thanks, also, for being the first to show me how a godly husband honors his wife.

Glenn Olson, my passion for ministering to teens is because of you. Thank you for modeling a life of intimacy with Christ, for equipping me to serve, and for being the biggest champion of my writing. I am so much of who I am because of you and Anne.

Centennial Church, you have been a family to me from the time you welcomed me as a college student. I can't begin to express how much I've been shaped by the community, teaching, friendships, and challenges of family life together. Thank you for trusting me to lead and allowing me to fail, learn, and try again.

To the whole EFCA: it's a joy and a gift to be part of this larger family of churches. God has used you to encourage my heart, instruct my mind, and enlarge my vision. In particular, the network of youth workers that meets in the Minneapolis west metro: you've been partners, prayer warriors, and encouragers. I pray this book will be a tool for our churches in our shared mission.

Laurie Seay, Justin Wevers, and the rest of the Challenge team: thank you for encouraging me to write this book and listening to me process through my fears of doing so.

To Kathy Linde, for so consistently praying over this project whenever I sent you a text. Your prayers were invaluable.

So many people reviewed some or all of this book and gave suggestions and input: Dave, David, Cody, Caleb, Laurie, Jon, Andrew, Luke, Christie, Lee, Rob, Kate, Jack, Kate, Justin, Tracy, Greg, Peter, Andrea, and Rachel. Thank you.

To my editor, Katy Morgan: I truly believe God brought you to this project! Your editing skills, thoughtful questions, and gracious push-back have made this book so much better than it would have been. Thank you for advocating for this book and working so hard on it. It's been a joy to work with you.

To all of my students through the years: thanks for allowing me to be a part of your lives, for sharing your stories and questions and struggles and joys. It's been a privilege to teach, to listen, and to walk alongside you. I hope I've represented your stories well, and I pray that God will use them. Thanks to my current group of middle-school girls for being so excited that I'm writing a book!

Elliana, Audrey, and Isaac: thanks for letting Mom hide in my room for hours on end so I could write. I love you each more than you'll ever know, and I pray that you grow up knowing Jesus as the best treasure you could find.

Greg, what can I say? You are servant-hearted, patient, tender, forgiving, passionate, self-sacrificing, and faithful. Being married to you has given me a daily, tangible picture of the love of Jesus—and brought so much joy. Thank you for the additional sacrifices you made for me to write this book, for being my sounding board for everything, for supporting me, and for reminding me of the gospel when I get stuck on something less. I still can't believe I get to do life with you.

And finally, to my Savior. Thank you for your boundless love, which I could never deserve. I hope this book honors you and shows others just a glimpse of how amazing you are. There is truly nothing that compares to knowing you.

FOR FURTHER READING

For those who would like to dive deeper into the topics of this book, here are a few helpful resources.

GENERAL SEXUALITY

Sam Allberry, *Why Does God Care Who I Sleep With?*

This book offers one of the most concise and convincing discussions of the reasons for the Bible's sexual ethic.

Juli Slattery, *Rethinking Sexuality*

Juli helps change the framework for how we think about and live out our sexuality—it's all to honor God.

Paul David Tripp, "10 Things You Should Know About Sex"

(www.crossway.org/articles/10-things-you-should-know-about-sex)

Short but powerful, this article sums up some of the most important principles for understanding sex from a biblical perspective.

Rooted, "Sex Education Curriculum for Families"

(www.rootedministry.com/sex-education-podcasts-parent-conversation-guide)

A podcast series introducing a biblical perspective on sexuality and offering discussion questions for parents and teens.

Christopher Yuan, *Holy Sexuality*

(www.holysexuality.com)

This 12-lesson video curriculum gives an overview of the Bible's teachings on sexuality in light of the gospel.

LGBTQ+ TOPICS

Jackie Hill Perry, *Gay Girl, Good God*

Telling the story of how she met Jesus as a lesbian and her journey of following Jesus, Jackie weaves in a lot of gospel theology regarding sin, sexuality, and discipleship.

Rachel Gilson, *Born Again This Way*

Rachel addresses many of the pressing questions of people wrestling with same-sex attraction, while sharing her own beautiful story.

Becket Cook, *A Change of Affection*

An honest account of how Becket, a successful set designer whose identity was all about being gay, came to be transformed by the gospel.

Preston Sprinkle, *Embodied*

This book seeks to graciously and biblically answer questions around transgender identities.

THE BODY

Sam Allberry, *What God Has to Say about Our Bodies*

This is for you if you want to know more about what the Bible teaches about our bodies, why they matter, and how God calls us to live in them.

PORN

Ray Ortlund, *The Death of Porn*

This gentle, hopeful book will help you see porn in light of justice, hope, and the gospel—and give you a vision for being part of the solution.

Heath Lambert, *Finally Free*

If you're looking for a gospel perspective and practical help for fighting a porn addiction, you'll find this book a great tool.

MARRIAGE & SINGLENESS

Christopher Ash, *Married for God*

A great overview of what the Bible has to say about what marriage is and why it matters.

Sam Allberry, *Seven Myths about Singleness*

This book addresses common misconceptions about being single and addresses them in light of the gospel.

ABUSE

Steven R. Tracy and others, *Mending the Soul: Student Edition*

If you've suffered abuse, this book helps you to understand what happened to you and points out a path toward healing through Jesus.

OTHER HARD QUESTIONS

Rebecca McLaughlin, *10 Questions Every Teen Should Ask (And Answer) About Christianity*

If you have questions about the Bible and science, morality, diversity, suffering, hell, and other difficult issues, this book will give you a good start in answering them.

INTIMACY WITH JESUS

Jaquelle Crow, *This Changes Everything*

Written by a teen for teens, this book will encourage you in the gospel and teach you practices for growing closer to Jesus.

Paul David Tripp, *New Morning Mercies*

A year's worth of short, gospel-centered devotions. I suggest combining it with reading the Bible each day. (Use his suggested passages, or start in John or Psalms.)

Discussion Guide

1. AN ETERNAL ECHO

- Was there anything in this chapter that you had never heard before? What did you think of it?

- Read Genesis 1:26-28 and 2:18-25. How many observations can you make from these passages about God's intention for marriage and sex?

- Why is marriage so central to the Bible's story? In what ways does it picture God?

- How does this change how we think about sex?

- If God designed sex to point us to him, and we leave him out of the picture, how will this affect our experience of sex?

2. AN ANCIENT LIE

- Where do you see or experience the world being broken?

- On a scale of 1 to 10, what is your level of confidence in God as the one who can best define and provide what is truly good? Can you say why?

- From God's perspective, what is sin? Why is it a big deal? Read Colossians 3:5 and Hebrews 3:12 to help you answer.

- What commands of God do you hear people questioning most often?

- In what ways are the sins we struggle with (sexual or not) about trust and reliance? About worship?

3. AN ULTIMATE HERO

- Did this chapter change how you think about Jesus? In what way?

- Read John 4:1-42 together. What did Jesus want for this woman? What did he mean when he offered her "living water"?

- Read John 17:20-26. What does Jesus' prayer for all believers reveal about what he most desires for us? How can we experience that more fully?

- What do you think it means to be united with Christ? What do you think it is like as an experience?

- How does someone say yes to Jesus? What does that involve? And what do you think most often keeps people from doing that?

4. BODY

- Read Genesis 1:26-27. What do you think it means to be made in God's image?

- Why is it significant that Jesus came to earth as an embodied human?

- Read Romans 12:1-2. What would it look like to offer both your body and mind to God in worship as a "living sacrifice"?

- Do you tend to focus more on your heart or your outward actions? What does Scripture say about the importance of each?

- To what degree do you think it is ok to attempt to change our bodies? (Hair dye? Piercings or tattoos? Corrective surgery? Plastic surgery? Gender affirmation surgery?) Where do we draw the line, biblically, and why? Does it depend on our motivations for these changes?

5. IDENTITY

- What do people around you tend to find their identity in? Have you seen someone's identity crumble when that part of them changed?

- Of the identities that God speaks over his followers (re-read the list of "second-layer identities" on page 58), which one speaks to you the most?

- Truth and reality are steady and dependable things separate from our feelings. How is this idea freeing?

- Read Psalm 139. How does it make you feel to think that God knows you better than you know yourself?

- If you had a friend who believed something about their identity that you thought was at odds with God's view of them—maybe about their weight or gender or value—how could you love them unconditionally without necessarily accepting their view of themselves?

6. DESIRE

- What is the good purpose of our sexual desires? What would God have us do with these desires while we're single?

- Read James 1:12-18 and 1 Peter 2:11. At what point does temptation become sin? Where does desire fit in? What promises and encouragements do these passages give us regarding temptations?

- How have you experienced God providing a way out from temptation? How can we help each other in this battle?

- What are some common temptations teens face? What's the original good desire beneath them, and how does Jesus want to satisfy those desires?

- How would you answer a friend who asks, "Doesn't God want me to be happy?"

7. GENDER

- How did this chapter change the way you think about gender? Was there anything you disagreed with?

- Read Genesis 1:27. How is our gender part of being made in the image of God?

- What is gender? What is its purpose?

- We read, *"Our culture talks about gender in terms of identity and expression—both individualistic categories, based on your inward feelings or on how you want to be seen by others. Biblically, though, our gender has been created by God in our bodies, and it's meant to be pointed outward and life-giving."* Without being a spouse or parent, how can someone's gender be a blessing to others? How can it be a reflection of God?

- What pronouns would you use for a trans friend? How did the questions on the previous page challenge you to make this decision more thoughtfully? Would you have a different answer in different situations? (Consider in person versus online, one-on-one settings versus publicly, or with a close friend versus a stranger.) What if it were legally required that you use a person's preferred pronouns?

8. SINGLENESS

- What words come to mind when you think of lifelong singleness? Did this chapter shift your perspective?

- Read 1 Corinthians 7. In what ways is singleness a gift? What makes it a better option than marriage for some?

- In what ways does singleness testify to the gospel? Have you seen that lived out by any single people you know?

- How has God designed the church to be a community, a family? Read Acts 2:42-47 as an example. What are some ways we can grow in being a better reflection of this, to ensure no one among us feels alone?

- In what situations in life is it hardest to be content? How can Jesus bring joy to those places?

9. INTIMACY

- What are some promises that our culture makes around "sexual freedom"? As you watch people around you, have you seen those promises delivered on over the long run?

- How would you explain to a friend why God commands us to reserve sex for marriage? Read 1 Corinthians 6:12-20. Why does what we do with our bodies matter to God?

- How do you feel hearing that *"choices do not guarantee outcomes"*? In what ways is that sobering? In what ways is it actually good news?

- What hope is there for those who've made sexual choices they regret? Read 1 Corinthians 6:9-11 to help you answer.

- What specific, practical means does Jesus give to us, both as individuals and in community with other believers, to help us draw closer to him and truly experience him as our greatest treasure and joy?

10. ORIENTATION

- What arguments have you heard against the Bible's teaching on sexuality? How does this chapter challenge what you've believed or felt about homosexuality?

- Read Romans 1:16-32. What do we exchange when we pursue homosexuality (or any form of ungodliness)? See also Hebrews 12:14-16.

- In what ways is homosexuality a distortion of God's design for sex? In what ways is it an issue of worship?

- How has the church mishandled this issue at times? What would it look like for your church to live out both love and truth toward the LGBTQ+ community?

- Specifically, what kind of culture and environment must we cultivate in our youth group and our church so that teenagers who are attracted to people of the same sex will find welcome and support as they seek to follow Jesus?

11. SCREENS

- Which of the reasons for avoiding porn did you find most convincing? Why?

- How do you usually hear porn talked about? How can you be a part of changing those conversations?

- Read Matthew 5:27-29. Why does Jesus take lust so seriously? Do you think he wants us to actually gouge out our eyes if they cause us to sin? If not, what does he mean?

- Read Romans 12:1-2 and 9-10. Even though Paul didn't have porn in mind when he penned these verses, how many principles can you find that apply to the topic?

- Do you have people who you can talk with about anything and who help you to follow Jesus? Who are they? How can we create an environment for more of these kinds of relationships in church?

12. DATING

- What is love? How would you define it? Read Ephesians 5:1-2. How does this adjust your definition?

- Read 1 Thessalonians 4:1-8. What goals or guidelines would you want to set up to help ensure a healthy dating relationship?

- How would you tell if a boyfriend or girlfriend is honoring you, causing no harm, and demonstrating self-control and holiness in the relationship?

- Why is it important that Christians date only other believers? Have you seen a Christian date a non-Christian? What did you observe about their relationship? Why do you think people are tempted to do this?

- Whether you're dating or not, what are some ways you can begin cultivating self-control and patience?

13. ABUSE

- Read Psalm 10:12-18. Why does God care so deeply about the abused and suffering? What do you notice about the psalmist's prayer in light of oppression and suffering?

- Do you know how you would you respond if a friend told you that she/he was dealing with abuse or had been assaulted?

- How can we as God's people reflect his heart for victims of abuse? Where could we connect them with real help?

- Read Isaiah 10:1-3. How is it good news that God is Judge and will call the wicked oppressors to account?

- Read Isaiah 61:1-7. What does God promise to his people who have suffered?

ON THE BOOK AS A WHOLE

- Having read the whole book, which chapter stands out to you? What did you learn from it?

- Are there any points from the book that you still disagree with or aren't sure about?

- How do you think your life will be different because of this study? What's one thing you would like to do because of what you learned?

- How would you answer a friend who asks, "What does the Bible say about sex?"

- Read Matthew 13:44. What has following Jesus required you to give up? (Or what would he require you to give up in order to follow him?) What does he offer that makes it worth it?

NOTES

1   Sam Allberry, *Why Does God Care Who I Sleep With?* (The Good Book Company, 2020), p 136.

2   Jackie Hill Perry, *Gay Girl, Good God* (B&H, 2018), p 18.

3   "What Do We Actually Know about Sexual Orientation? Part 2," The Center for Faith, Sexuality, and Gender (August 16, 2018): www.centerforfaith.com/blog/what-do-we-actually-know-about-sexual-orientation-part-2 (accessed December 1, 2022).

4   Jackie Hill Perry, *Gay Girl, Good God*, p 109.

5   Sam Allberry, *Is God Anti-Gay?* (Second edition: The Good Book Company, 2023), p 60.

6   C.S. Lewis, *The Weight of Glory* (HarperOne, 2001; first published 1949), p 26.

7   Rachel Gilson, *Born Again This Way* (The Good Book Company, 2020), p 70.

8   Paul R. McHugh and Lawrence S. Mayer, "Sexuality and Gender: Findings from the Biological, Psychological, and Social Sciences," *New Atlantis* No. 50 (Fall 2016), p 90. Quoted in Preston Sprinkle, *Embodied* (David C. Cook, 2021), p 38.

9   Mark Yarhouse, *Understanding Gender Dysphoria* (IVP, 2015), p 17.

10 www.plannedparenthood.org/learn/gender-identity/sex-gender-identity (accessed May 26, 2023).

11 Tim and Kathy Keller, *The Meaning of Marriage* (Dutton, 2011), p 186.

12 I took this image from Tim and Kathy Keller's book *The Meaning of Marriage*, p 174.

13 A helpful article for thinking through disability through the lens of Scripture can be found here: www.thegospelcoalition.org/article/is-disability-normal (accessed April 18, 2023).

14 Jackie Hill Perry, *Gay Girl, Good God*, p 110-111.

15 Russell B. Toomey, Amy K. Syvertsen, and Maura Shramko, "Transgender Adolescent Suicide Behavior," *Pediatrics*, volume 2, issue 4 (October 2018): publications.aap.org/pediatrics/

article/142/4/e20174218/76767/Transgender-Adolescent-Suicide-Behavior (accessed March 10, 2023).

16 For example:
J. D. Greear, "When talking with a transgender person, which pronoun should you use?" (November 18, 2019): jdgreear.com/podcasts/when-talking-with-a-transgender-person-which-pronoun-should-you-use (accessed March 10, 2022).
Preston Sprinkle, *Embodied*, p 212.
Mark Yarhouse, "Understanding the Transgender Phenomenon," *Christianity Today* (June 8, 2015): www.christianitytoday.com/ct/2015/july-august/understanding-transgender-gender-dysphoria.html (accessed March 10, 2022).

17 For example:
John Piper, "He or She? How Should I Refer to Transgender Friends?" (July 16, 2015): www.desiringgod.org/interviews/he-or-she-how-should-i-refer-to-transgender-friends (accessed March 10, 2022).
Andrew Walker, "He, She, Ze, Zir? Navigating pronouns while loving your transgender neighbour" (August 31, 2018): www.thegoodbook.co.uk/blog/interestingthoughts/2018/08/31/he-she-ze-zir-navigating-pronouns-while-loving-you (accessed March 10, 2022).
Denny Burk, "Bruce or Caitlyn? He or she? Should Christians accommodate transgender naming?" (June 4, 2015): www.dennyburk.com/bruce-or-caitlyn-he-or-she-should-christians-accomodate-transgender-naming (accessed March 10, 2022).

18 For example, Sam Allberry, "Should I Call Someone by Their Preferred Pronouns?" (April 10, 2019): www.youtube.com/watch?v=4ur-lfYF4dc (accessed March 10, 2022).

19 Becket Cook, *A Change of Affection* (Thomas Nelson, 2019), p 108.

20 Sam Allberry, "How Both Singleness and Marriage Testify to the Gospel" (March 10, 2019): www.crossway.org/articles/how-both-singleness-and-marriage-testify-to-the-gospel (accessed May 8, 2022).

21 Sarah Eekhoff Zylstra and Colin Hansen, "Unmarried Sex Is Worse Than You Think" (August 17, 2021): www.thegospelcoalition.org/article/unmarried-sex-worse (accessed May 8, 2022).

22 Noam Shpancer, "How Many Sex Partners Does It Really Take to Be Happy?" (*Psychology Today*, May 13, 2016): www.psychologytoday.com/us/blog/insight-therapy/201605/how-many-sex-partners-

does-it-really-take-be-happy (accessed April 18, 2023).

23 Justin Garcia, Chris Reiber, Sean G. Massey, and Ann M. Merriwether, "Sexual Hook-Up Culture," *American Psychological Association*, volume 44, no. 2 (February, 2013): www.apa.org/monitor/2013/02/ce-corner (accessed April 18, 2023).

24 Theresa E. Donato, "Are Couples Who Live Together Before Marriage More Likely to Divorce?", *Psychology Today* (January 27, 2021): www.psychologytoday.com/us/blog/meet-catch-and-keep/202101/is-living-together-marriage-associated-divorce (accessed April 18, 2023).

25 Nicholas H. Wolfinger, "Does Sexual History Affect Marital Happiness?" (October 22, 2018): www.ifstudies.org/blog/does-sexual-history-affect-marital-happiness (accessed February 23, 2023).

26 Daniel B. Wallace, "Review of Mel White's 'What the Bible Says— and Doesn't Say—about Homosexuality'" (November 6, 2006): www.bible.org/article/review-mel-white-s-what-bible-says-and-doesn-t-say-about-homosexuality (accessed February 28, 2023).

27 Listen to his story on his website: www.christopheryuan.com/videos.

28 Matthew Vines, "The Gay Debate" (March 10, 2012): www.matthewvines.com/transcript (accessed October 7, 2022).

29 Ed Shaw, *Purposeful Sexuality* (IVP, 2021), p 30.

30 See Sam Allberry, *Why Does God Care Who I Sleep With?*, p 18.

31 Keith Rose, "Porn and Sex Trafficking: Is There a Connection?" (December 15, 2022): www.covenanteyes.com/2011/09/07/the-connections-between-pornography-and-sex-trafficking (accessed October 14, 2022).

32 Brian Y. Park et al., "Is Internet Ponography Causing Sexual Dysfunctions? A Review with Clinical Reports," *Behavioural Sciences* volume 6, no. 3 (September 2016): www.ncbi.nlm.nih.gov/pmc/articles/PMC5039517 (accessed February 25, 2022).

33 Whitney L. Rostad et al., "The Association Between Exposure to Violent Pornography and Teen Dating Violence in Grade 10 High School Students," *Archives of Sexual Behavior*, volume 48, no. 7 (October, 2019): www.ncbi.nlm.nih.gov/pmc/articles/PMC6751001 (accessed February 25, 2022).

34 Christina Camilleri et al., "Compulsive Internet Pornography Use and Mental Health: A Cross-Sectional Study in a Sample of University Students in the United States," *Frontiers in Psychology*,

volume   11   (2020):   www.ncbi.nlm.nih.gov/pmc/articles/
PMC7835260 (accessed February 25, 2023).

35   Tim Keller, *The Prodigal Prophet* (Viking, 2018), p 58.

36   Jared Kennedy, *A Parent's Guide to Teaching Your Children about Gender* (Leland House, 2020), p 28.

37   www.cdc.gov/violenceprevention/childsexualabuse/fastfact.html (accessed October 14, 2022).

38   Sam Allberry, *Why Does God Care Who I Sleep With?*, p 136.

39   www.rainn.org/articles/child-sexual-abuse (accessed March 10, 2023).

40   J.D. Greear, "Downplaying the Sin of Homosexuality Won't Win the Next Generation" (February 9, 2023): www.thegospelcoalition.org/article/downplay-homosexual-sin-generation   (accessed February 14, 2023).

BIBLICAL | RELEVANT | ACCESSIBLE

At The Good Book Company, we are dedicated to helping Christians and local churches grow. We believe that God's growth process always starts with hearing clearly what he has said to us through his timeless word—the Bible.

Ever since we opened our doors in 1991, we have been striving to produce Bible-based resources that bring glory to God. We have grown to become an international provider of user-friendly resources to the Christian community, with believers of all backgrounds and denominations using our books, Bible studies, devotionals, evangelistic resources, and DVD-based courses.

We want to equip ordinary Christians to live for Christ day by day, and churches to grow in their knowledge of God, their love for one another, and the effectiveness of their outreach.

Call us for a discussion of your needs or visit one of our local websites for more information on the resources and services we provide.

Your friends at The Good Book Company

thegoodbook.com | thegoodbook.co.uk
thegoodbook.com.au | thegoodbook.co.nz
thegoodbook.co.in